DIVINE ENCOUNTERS
of a
SERVANT'S HEART

DIVINE ENCOUNTERS
of a
SERVANT'S HEART

Choosing to obey GOD,
even when it makes you uncomfortable

GLENDA J. JOHNSTON

XULON PRESS

Xulon Press
2301 Lucien Way #415
Maitland, FL 32751
407.339.4217
www.xulonpress.com

Edited by Xulon Press

Printed in the United States of America.

ISBN-13: 9781545616031

Dedication

I DEDICATE THIS BOOK TO my husband, Danny, the love of my life, who has always been there. He has always allowed me to follow wherever and whatever the LORD said, and he has been on many of these divine encounters, right by my side, to stand strong by me whatever the plan was for our life. To our sons, Danny Joe and J.W., who have always been my greatest supporters, for always believing in me, and to our blessed family that believes in me and loves the LORD CHRIST JESUS, may we always serve HIM and keep the family that GOD has given us together!

Contents

Divine Encounters of a Servant's Heart

CHOOSING TO OBEY GOD Even When It Makes You Uncomfortable or Does Not Seem Right to You

I was saved at the age of twelve years. At that time I did not understanding discernment, but I had a very strong feeling that something was leading me to know things and to pray for others; it seemed like I knew their needs or even felt their hurt and loneliness. I loved the word in Psalm 139:23 (NIV): "Search me, GOD, and know my heart, test me and know my anxious thoughts." I felt many times that JESUS was telling me things and directing my life. At the age of fourteen, while attending church camp, I felt the leading of the HOLY SPIRIT showing me what JESUS wanted for my life, and later that year, it became very clear to me how I had received the beautiful gift JESUS gave me in discernment. I started listening with an open heart and an ear for HIS voice to direct my steps. This book contains just some of the divine encounters that I experienced from 1979 to 2017, following HIS voice. I'm very thankful for these divine encounters and the LORD allowing this vessel to be used. It has caused me to grow in HIS word and to strengthen my faith and to believe in HIS miracles! These are true divine encounters with the HOLY SPIRIT directing my footsteps all the way, for it is never easy to be compliant and obey the call when you feel uncomfortable moving out of your comfort zone, but I'm very thankful for listening and responding to HIS call and never being so busy with my life that I did not give the time to go where HE said to go, even though many times I would say, "Really, LORD, you want me to do what?" Thank YOU, JESUS for not giving up on me as a vessel for YOU. Thank You, LORD JESUS, for YOUR direction, as I tried to always obey, but there were times I was not hearing you as carefully as I should have, I wasn't going where you wanted, or I just wasn't standing on YOUR word, but thank YOU, GOD, for never giving up on me.

The Bible talks about divine appointments, favor, and encounters. My prayer is to always be ready to be used when HE calls. May I grow stronger in hearing and acting at the first sound of HIS voice and that I may always move in the direction HE leads. My prayer for those who read this book is to ask the LORD to use you as a vessel that is willing to do HIS work and see the Kingdom advance. Then it is time for you to listen and move. One thing I've learned over the years is GOD is faithful even when we are not; HE'S a restoring GOD, a healing

GOD, and a supplier of all our needs. Read Philippians 4:19. As I wrote this book, I have added some short devotions in the back that the LORD gives me daily that I have called "Food for Thought." I trust this book will kindle a fire in you for JESUS and HIS divine encounters for your life, and may they bless you as they have me, for JESUS feeds me daily with HIS words.

Chapter 1

The Dream

A FTER DANNY HAD LEFT for Vietnam and was there a few months, one of the old saints in His mom and dad's church, Sister Hanes, sent me a letter and Danny a postcard; she said she had been praying for protection over Danny that evening and later went on to bed. Sister Hanes said, "I was awakened up out of a dream, and I saw Danny like the baby Moses. Danny was in a basket and floating in the water." She said she heard the LORD say, "Danny will be kept safe; just as baby Moses was spared, so will Danny. He will come home safe!" Well, Sister Hanes said she got down on her knees and thanked the LORD for the vision in the dream and started writing both of us. She wanted us to know that Danny was going to be okay. I thank GOD for the people who truly pray for others, for listening to their prayers, and for making Sister Hanes a willing vessel to tell it.

Danny was given a prayer cloth just before he left for Vietnam that his Dad and Mother and their church had prayed over. To this day Danny still carries it in his billfold, and it represents a point of contact from so many to him. I'm thankful that the LORD was not finished with Danny. Several years later Danny was saved and baptized with our older son, which was such a blessing. Danny has always been such a strong tower for me, and many times I've had to be for him. This shows us just how GOD uses people in your life, so when you pray, do not give up. Your prayers are being heard, and the answer is coming. We have to wait on HIS time. Remember the Bible says, "Our thoughts are not like HIS and our ways are not like HIS ways, so hold on for HE is a good, good GOD." Read Isaiah 55:8 KJV. "For my thoughts are not your thoughts, neither are your ways MY ways, saith the LORD." Over the years we have learned the power of prayer, and we are thankful for others who still pray for us. I always want to be a child of our living LORD JESUS, one just like Sister Hanes who knew the LORD and knew when HE would show you through a dream or vision for someone else and to know HIS voice that close that you have to go and share the dream with the one it is about.

Chapter 2

A Child Returns Home

I T WAS A REGULAR Wednesday night, and I was supposed to sing a special, so I was getting ready to go up and stand by the piano to sing. As I got up, our pastor said, "Let's pray," and as he prayed, the LORD spoke to me and said, "Leave right now, and go to this house." As usual, I did not have my purse, so that meant I had no car keys. Our boys sat between us, and we were in the front pew, so I was trying to get my husband's attention to give me his car keys. Well, I realized at this time how many people did not close their eyes when we pray because it seemed like everyone saw me leave the church, and I was trying to leave without causing a big distraction. When I got outside the church, I felt the HOLY SPIRIT was moving me very quickly, and I was feeling a little crazy. I asked the LORD, "What is it you want me to do?" In a voice as strong as could be, I heard Him say, "Go down this road, and stop at this house, and go in!"

Well, when I drove down that road and stopped in front of the house, I begged the LORD, "Please, do not make me knock on this door and go in." You see, I knew this family very well, and I even asked GOD to not let them be home (remember, when GOD asks you to do something, you may be like me and feel silly). As I got out of the car, walking up to the door, I still asked GOD for them not to be home. I felt that they would think how silly for me to be saying the LORD sent me here. But I heard the HOLY SPIRIT say, "Get in there—now," so I knocked on the door, praying still that no one would answer. I turned to go back to my car, asking the LORD for no one to be home, when the door opened, and a young lady was standing there whom I did not know. She said, "Can I help you?"

I replied, "I need to see John." She said that he was eating and that I would have to come back at another time. About that time I heard the HOLY SPIRIT say, "You have to see Him now!" I knew this house well—I had been there many times in the past years—and I knew this man very well, so I said, "I have to see Him now" and turned to go up a few steps to the kitchen. As I turned the corner, there sat John choking on a piece of ham he was trying to eat. I laid my hands on His shoulder and said, "In the name of JESUS, unchoke now." At that moment he coughed up and spit out a small piece of ham. I later found out that John had throat cancer. At that moment, I noticed the young lady had a look of shock and amazement all in one and was crying.

I hugged John and the young lady, said good-bye, and went back to church. As I shared what had happened, I found out he had a lot of family in our church, and they all cried and rejoiced. As time went by, not thinking about this divine encounter, I read in the newspaper that John had passed away. So my husband and I went to the funeral home, and as we started up the stairs, a young woman open the door to greet us and said, "There's that angel I saw that night." She then told us that she had walked away from the LORD, years earlier, that her dad was a preacher, and that after I left the night John was choking, she fell on her knees and came back to JESUS. Now you see why I called this chapter "A Child Returns Home." I truly believe it was for her that the LORD sent me there. I know HE knew this child needed to repent and start serving HIM again!

That is why it is important to move as the LORD asks you to. I praise GOD for allowing me to be part of HIS plan, in hearing from this prodigal child that she returned back to JESUS. When she told us about her asking the LORD to forgive her and that she wanted the LORD back in her life again, it made me think about the parable in Luke 15:11–32 (KJV). Take time to read it, and pray for those who have not returned.

Chapter 3

Knowing HIS Voice

THERE WAS A RULE between my husband and me, when our boys were out late, he was always to answer the phone at night, not me. It just happened one night that I had gone to bed early, and our youngest son woke me up by calling out his brother's name and saying, "What do you want, Danny?" This caused me to get out of my bed and go see what he was talking about, but he was sound asleep. I then started to the kitchen, and the phone rang. My husband was asleep in his chair, so without a thought I answered the phone. Our older son said, "Mom, I've had an accident. I'm okay, but my girlfriend is hurt a little, bloody nose." He said it happened on the Johnston City blacktop, and I told him we would be right there and hung up.

I woke my husband up and told him what had happened and that we needed to go there. Well, as we started out the door, my husband asked me where on the blacktop were they, and I said somewhere on the Johnston City blacktop. Exactly at that time I heard the HOLY SPIRIT say, "I will lead you to him." Later, as my husband drove us to the Johnston City blacktop, I heard the HOLY SPIRIT again tell me to turn here and go up to this house on the hill. Another amazing thing was the lady in this house said, "My husband works nights, and I do not answer the door to anyone after dark! I would have never opened the door to your son, but I heard the LORD say, "Let them in."

The next morning I asked our younger son if he remembered calling out his brother's name, and he said, yes. Then I asked him what he wanted, but he never answered me. I believe this was why the LORD woke me up, to be ready for the call, so you see why we must listen to HIS voice. I'm so very thankful for people like this lady who listened to JESUS and opened the door for our son and his girlfriend. She also told me she knew it was GOD because she said she knew our son never told us exactly where he was and we showed up. She said to me, "It sure made me know how wonderful GOD works. You see, where this accident happened, no one would have seen his truck down in that ditch, and it was not close to any town or phone." I thank God for knowing and hearing from the guidance's of the HOLY SPIRIT and trusting and obeying His words.

Chapter 4

GOD Sent Help

HAVE YOU EVER GONE to look at new vehicles and got bitten by the bug so badly that you had to have them? Well, we did; we bought two new vehicles: a truck and a car (I hope I never get up on that side of the bed ever again, ha-ha).It was time for the car to be serviced. We had bought them in Vienna, Illinois, which was about one hour and forty minutes from home. I took the car down that morning, and they gave me a loner car to drive for a few days. A few days later, I got the call that we could pick up the car, so I called a good dear friend and asked her if she would like to ride along with me, and she said yes. The next day I picked her up, and we started to drive to Vienna, which was a little over an hour drive and very hilly. As we were driving, the car started making a funny sound and acting like it could not get enough gas.

My friend said to me, "It acts like it's almost out of gas." I looked down at the gas gauge and said, "No, it shows it has plenty, a little over a fourth of a tank." Well, by this time, we were way out in the countryside, and it started getting worse, so I started praying. Back then there were no cell phones, and there were no houses close that we could see. We were too far from the town we had gone through earlier to turn around. We felt lost and didn't know what to do, but I began praying, and as I prayed, we would go a little farther and then almost stop. I said again, as I laid hands on the dash, "In the name of JESUS, go," and we would, but then it was trying to come to a complete stop.

My friend said, "We are out of gas. I know because I have run out of gas before," and I said to her, "Please stop saying we are out of gas; pray, and do not be a doubting Thomas. If we stop, you have to get out and push." We had to laugh or we both would have been crying. Each time we prayed, we went a little farther, but all of a sudden, we came to a dead stop. She got out and pushed us over to the side of the road by a shade tree. Did I mention it was 100 degrees in the shade that day? We sat there wondering what we could do and praying that the LORD would send someone.

It seemed that day no one was even on the road. We talked about trying to walk, but I said it was too hot. So, we sat there, prayed, and talked. A few minutes after we prayed, a car came up behind us, and a woman got out and said, "I know you are out of gas." She put gas in the car, but before we could thank her, she was gone. My friend and I were amazed and believed we were entertained by an angel. We got back in the car, and it started right up. For the rest of the drive there, all we could do was talk about this lady: what had happened and who she was. When we got to the garage, we started telling the owner of the garage about what had happened and tried to describe the lady and her car to see if he knew her because he knew everyone in the small town. I knew he loved the LORD and would understand this. No one seemed to know the lady or the car. Then one of his workers in the back of the garage came to his office and said, "I do not know how they drove this car here!" He looked as if he were in shock. Scratching his head, he said, "This car is a fuel-injection car, and just adding gas to it would not have caused this car to go!" My friend and I and the owner of the garage just looked at each other, and I said "It was an angel!" Well, we all just praised the LORD for us getting there without the use of gas. All I can say is, the angel appeared to make us think the gas would make us go, but now I know the prayers were heard, and the power of the LORD carried us!

Chapter 5

Just Asleep

M Y HUSBAND WAS A coal miner in southern Illinois and was hurt underground. He injured his back, and later that week, he had to have back surgery. After a long stay in the hospital, he came home, but after a few weeks home, I had to take him back to the emergency room at the hospital in Evansville because he was having trouble breathing. They said he had pleurisy, an inflammation of the tissue layers lining the lung and inner chest wall, and sent us back home with new medication. Well, by morning he was worse. We did not sleep at all that night. He could not sit back or lay back because he could not breathe and was in severe pain, gasping every breath.

Early the next morning, I took him to our ER at Farrell Hospital, and our family doctor saw him right away. He did x-rays and said, "I feel he has blood clots in the lungs and is critical" and called for the helicopter from St. Mary's Hospital to come and life-flight Danny back to Evansville, Indiana. Our doctor told me that he did not think Danny would live, so I told his mom and dad so they could go with me. His Dad did not want to go at that moment. Later I found out his dad just wanted to be alone with the LORD and pray for his son to live. So his mother went with me, and when we got to the hospital, all the doctors said in the ICU was that Danny was not going to make it.

They said his lungs were full of blood clots, so we knew we needed to call his sister, who lived out of state, to come to the hospital. She then stayed with her mom and dad and helped take care of the boys and also brought her mom back and forth to the hospital while the boys were in school, so I could stay with Danny and not leave him. Danny's sister's husband, Jim, stayed back home with their two small children. Jim said he felt compelled to get up on Sunday morning to go to a strange church (they had just moved there) with two small babies and put them in a strange nursery. When he went into the sanctuary, the preacher said, "There is someone here that needs to stand in the gap for a dying man," so Jim stepped out and went down, and they laid hands on Him for Danny. Jim sent Danny a letter telling Him about this.

That same night the Lord woke up my friend from Eldorado, who has a medical condition (seizures) in which she should not be awakened suddenly, said she heard me say, "The boys' dad is dying." She woke up her husband, and they got on their knees and prayed. She called the ICU trying to get me, but they never let me know. Danny's dad prayed for the LORD to leave Danny and take him, and he knew the exact time the LORD touched Danny with His healing power. Later Danny's dad told me the exact time that Danny was healed.

I was sitting at the foot of Danny's bed when all the machines went off, indicating that Danny had passed away. In just that second, there were nurses and doctors coming into Danny's room. One of the doctors came in and said to the nurse that I needed to step out for a moment, but I would not go out for I could hear the song Danny and I sang, "I have no fear when JESUS walks beside me, for I'm sheltered in the arms, the arms of GOD." I heard the LORD say, "He is just sleeping." Well, when I said, "He was just sleeping," one of the doctors said, "She is in shock. Please take her out now." Again I said no, and within seconds, all machines showed he was well and stable.

One of Danny's doctors, who was a lung specialist, came out of Danny's room and walked down the hall, telling other doctors he had just seen a miracle, and "HE did a hell of a job 'doing it'!" I thought this doctor was the one in shock, for I knew and believed in the healing power of JESUS. In just a few days, he was home and in the coming month had a fol-low-up appointment with the lung specialist and the back sur-geon. Both were still amazed at this miracle, and they both said, "What a great healing he had received." I'm so thankful for all these people, including his dad, our friend, and his brother-in-love, who heard from the LORD and reacted to HIS call on Danny's behalf. So everyone who reads this, keep your ears open to hear the FATHER, for HE may need your help in helping someone else somewhere. HE needs HIS vessels to work through at times, and we know HE loves HIS children and will call for you to serve HIM and others. The scripture James 5:16–17 (KJV) says, This is how I said it; prayers of the righteous man shall be heard!

Chapter 6

In the Time of Need

MY HUSBAND INJURED HIS back at work in the coal mines and had to have back surgery. We were sent to Saint Mary's Hospital in Evansville, Indiana. Danny was put in the hospital, and the next day they did His surgery. The doctor who did Danny's surgery really did not know us at all because this was an emergency surgery. They also kept Danny sedated for thirteen days, so he would not move and mess His back up. This was a very severe surgery. After Danny had been there a few days, one day at around six in the evening, His hospital door opened, and the doctor who had done Danny's surgery was standing in the doorway. All he said was, "I need you to talk to the MAN upstairs."

He never told me anything else, and I said okay. He closed the door and was gone. Danny was in a deep sleep from the sedation, and I knelt by His bed and held His hand and prayed for whatever was going on in this doctor's life at this moment, not knowing how or what to pray for, so I just prayed in the SPIRIT. I said to the LORD, "YOU know all and see all. Whatever is going on right now, I'm asking YOU for YOUR healing power to take over in this situation right now, in JESUS' name. Amen." A few hours later the door opened, and the doctor came in and said, "Thank you, thank you! My wife is okay, and so is our newborn daughter," and he left.

The next day I asked our nurse if she knew what had happened in this doctor's life last night, and she said yes. Then she told me that it was a touch-and-go situation in the birth of their first child on whether either mother or baby would live. So again I said, "Thank YOU, JESUS, for allowing us to be in this place, on this divine appointment for this doctor to feel YOUR presence in us and believe we could touch heaven for Him and His family." I thanked the LORD that HE allowed us to be part of such a blessing. I thanked the LORD that he moved this doctor to call out for prayer and to believe that we would pray. I'm thankful for being there at that time for Him and His family.

Years later we were sent to Him for Danny's shoulder surgery, but he could not do it, and before we left I said, "I know how old your oldest daughter is: thirty years old." He said, "How did you know?" and I shared who we were. He hugged me and smiled and said, "You are right." I again thanked GOD for allowing us to be there for them. My thoughts are, when you ask GOD to use you, you sure better be ready for where that might take you, for you have to be there in the time of need.

Chapter 7

Just Enough

WHEN DANNY WAS RECUPERATING from His back surgery, money became very short. I worked part time at the school in our hometown. One month I knew we would not have enough money to pay the monthly bills and buy food, but not wanting to add to Danny's stress, I chose not to tell Him. This was a very emotional time for Him, and he needed to recover. Yes I could have gone to family, but I did not want to do that because I knew it would upset Danny. He always was an outstanding provider for us! So I did the only thing I knew to do, and that was pray over this and leave it. Later that day, I heard the LORD say, "Trust ME," so I wrote the amount on a piece of paper and put it in a safe place where only I knew it was and no one else could see it.

Several days went by, and my grandmother Sarah would come and sit with Danny while I worked. She had just left, and Danny was in the backyard. He had just finished up walking around the yard, and as I came around the corner of the house,

Danny walked up to me and said, "You are not going to believe what happened this morning." He said a lady came to the door and said, "A long time ago you did some work for me, and I failed to pay you for it, so she gave Danny the exact amount we needed." I broke out crying and praising the LORD. Then I went into the house, got the paper, which was dated, and showed it to Danny. Then he cried, too—tears of joy!

I wished I could have always been that strong in my walk with the LORD, for as I write this, I recall that HE will always supply the need! Read Philippians 4:19 (KJV). My prayer for those that read this is that you just believe when things do not seem as if HE is not listening. The answer is coming, but we have to stand and believe in every word HE speaks, for HE will supply all we need in HIS right timing. Hang in there, my precious children, for joy truly does come in the morning. Amen.

Chapter 8

There All the Time

ONE FALL MORNING ABOUT ten, I was sitting on the couch and was sick. Well, it did not help that it was a very cloudy day, so that added to me feeling a little blue. I tried to get up and do some things around the house but found myself back on the couch, looking out the window and praying. It got to where I really did not know how to pray any longer, so I just sat there in the quietness of the room. The TV was off, and I did not even have a radio on, just waiting on the LORD to answer my prayer to feel better. Several hours went by, and the clouds were very dark over our house. Then the rain came, and the wind was blowing. Our boys were at school.

As I sat there all the sudden it was like Heaven opened up, and I felt the heat from the LORD's hand touch me. My whole body went from feeling cold to extremely warm, and it was like a bright light filled my living room. The sweetest peace came over me, and I knew I was healed. Well, a few days later, I was driving to St. Louis, Missouri, and I was praying for the

HOLY SPIRIT to come into my life with a prayer language with speaking in tongues, and I had the same experience as in my living room. I had to pull over the side of the road and stop, and I felt the touch on the top of my head all way down to my feet. There was the same bright light in my car that came through the front windshield and filled my car, and again it was cloudy and raining outside of my car.

From that day on I have realized just how wonderful JESUS is and how much HE wants to be with HIS children. I so wanted to be used by the LORD and to be able to pray for others, so I knew I needed the HOLY SPIRIT to lead me and to pray for me. At that time, so many Bible verses came to me, but the two that really stood out are John 14:18–19 (KJV): "I will not leave you comfortless: I will come to you. Yet a little while, and the world seeth me no more; but ye see me: because I live, ye shall live also" and Romans 8:26 (KJV): "Likewise the SPIRIT also helpeth our infirmities: for we know not what we should pray for as we ought: but the SPIRIT itself maketh intercession for us with groaning which cannot be uttered." If you love JESUS as HE loves you, allow HIM to use you and sit a while and allow HIM to come sit with you. Since this day I have had many divine appointments, and the encounters have been such an amazing blessing in my life and my family's lives also, as well as many other people's lives, so I pray as you read this that you're blessed.

Chapter 9

The Right Amount

ONE DAY, I WAS to pick up an associate and go do some appointments. That morning, the LORD told me in prayer what to do for her. Well, I was very uncomfortable about it, so I said to the LORD that I felt she would be offended with me or that I was trying to pry into her personal business. See how the evil one tries to destroy the good that GOD wants us to do? Well, the first appointment was at 1:30 p.m., so I picked her up, we left her car in the parking lot, and we drove to the appointment. It went very well. By the time we left that appointment, it was time for the next one, and as we were driving there, I felt the LORD say, "Talk to her and share what I told you to do this morning," but every time I started to share this word, either her phone would ring or mine, and then we were already at the next appointment.

This went on all afternoon. Finally it was 6:00 p.m. and time to take her back to her car so both of us could go home. As we drove back, we talked about how the day went and about our families and what we were doing this weekend, and by this time we were back to her car. I was hoping she would just get out of my car and be on her way home. So I pulled up to her car, and she opened the door and said, "See you Monday," and I said, "See you" and started to drive off. As I pulled out of the parking lot, I looked back and noticed she was still sitting there in her car. I again heard the LORD say, "Go back, and tell her what I said for you to do."

I turned around and pulled up beside her and, to my surprise, found out she was crying. I asked her to get back in my car and handed her the money the LORD had told me to give her, and then I told her what the LORD had said—that I should do this and tell her how much HE loves her and that He heard her prayer. Well, now she was really bawling, and I was bawling, too. She tried to tell me about her praying, but she just could not stop crying. Finally, she was able, through the tears, to tell me that she had been praying for the LORD to supply her with this exact amount of money. This is how much they were short for the house payment. I cried and said HE is always faithful in the time of need.

I also had to say, "Sorry, LORD, for not being more obedient sooner, for she would not have had to be so upset and would have seen that YOU did answer her prayers." By now she was crying and laughing, and I was, too. We both felt so much joy in our hearts. This was quite a lesson to me, that sometimes the one who is to be the messenger can fail the LORD and fail the person who was to be blessed. I'm very thankful that the LORD did not give up on me, being the messenger, for I was the one who truly received the blessing. So please listen and obey when the LORD needs you to be the messenger for HIM; remember we are the hands and feet of JESUS.

Chapter 10

The Stop Sign

ONE WEEKEND, AN ASSOCIATE Jackie and I traveled to Anderson, Indiana, to show her aunt the business that she was in, which was Primerica. We got there around five in the evening on that Friday. Her aunt had dinner waiting for us, so we ate and set up for a couple hours talking and then went to bed. The next morning after breakfast, we shared with her aunt what the business had to offer families and individuals. She really thought this business could help her church family, so we talked about doing seminars for the church. Later that day we visited the church and several places in Anderson, and then it was time to start home, so we thanked her aunt for having us and showing us around Anderson. We told her we had such a great time and she said that her niece would get back with her on a later date. We said our good-byes and started home. This was Saturday late afternoon.

On the way home, we talked a lot about the LORD and how great he was. Her aunt was in the ministry, and her uncle, who was deceased, had been the pastor of the church we were at. Her aunt shared with us just how great GOD was and how HE was taking care of her since her husband passed away. Jackie loved both of them so much, so the longer we drove, the more I could tell that the LORD was dealing with Jackie's heart. I shared on how easy it was to be saved: ask JESUS to forgive your sins and come into your heart and be your Savior, for the Bible says, "And everyone who calls on the name of the LORD will be saved" (Acts 2:21 NIV). I added, "It's that easy."

Well, it soon became time to stop and eat dinner, so we pulled into the parking lot of a restaurant, got out the car and went in. We ordered our meal, and all of a sudden, her tears started flowing. She was crying so hard that we could not even eat our meal, so we asked for our check, got back in the car, and headed home. We again talked about the LORD, and within a few hours, we arrived at my home. I hugged her and said, "Are you sure you're okay?" She said yes, so we said our good-byes, and off she drove to go to her home, which was about ninety minutes away. All night long, I kept on waking up and praying for her—she was so heavy on my mind. I asked the LORD to deal with her and allow her to open her heart to HIM. It sure seemed like a long, long night.

The next morning she called me and told me that she got up to the stop sign at the end of our road and cried out to the LORD to forgive her sins and save her, and she said,

"I'm saved and feel so good." Well, we both cried for joy, and what an amazing change I saw in her! I thanked the LORD for bringing her into my business and allowing us to become such great friends and for allowing me to share the love of JESUS with her and seeing her saved and working for the LORD. So many times as I prayed for her and her family, the LORD would ask me to tell her something specific, and each time I would feel very uncomfortable about it. My flesh did not want to always obey, but the HOLY SPIRIT knew better, so I would always tell her what the LORD said, and it always was the right time. She said, "I needed to hear this" or she would say, "This was an answer to the prayer I had been praying." I have learned that when GOD wants to use you, HE will get your attention, and I'm so thankful for HIM using me and being patient with me as I learn daily to obey.

Chapter 11

Wanted to Know

A S MANY OF YOU do daily, I was praying for family and friends. This evening I was praying for my Dad. He had been put in the VA hospital, and I had not gone to see Him yet. They thought he might have pneumonia, and that evening one of our boys had a basketball game, so that's where we were when Mom called me and left me a message to call her back. I called Mom, and she said that they thought Dad had pneumonia but were not sure and that she would go back with my sister tomorrow to see Him. I told her I would try to get up there some time in the next two days due to the boys' games. My husband was on second shift in the coal mines at this time, so I had to take them. So at this point, all I could do was pray.

My husband got home around midnight, and I had just gone to bed about eleven at night. Around three in the morning, the LORD woke me up and said that I needed to go see my dad, so I got out of bed and got dressed. Then I wrote a note to let my husband know where I had gone and that I would be back in time for church. As I drove to the Marion, Illinois, VA hospital, all I could do was pray. I did not have a scared feeling but just an urge to see Dad. Well, when I got there, I realized I did not even have the room Dad was in, so how was I to get in? I went to the ER and asked if I could go up into the hospital. Now you have to realize that back then, the hospitals were not as easy to enter as they are today at night.

One of the male nurses asked me who I wanted to see, so I told him my dad's name. He said that my dad was in a room with another man, and the floor nurse may say not right now and tell me to come back during visiting hours. However, the LORD was in this, and the floor nurses said, "Yes, send her on up." Away I went, and when I got to Dad's room, he was sitting on the side of his bed. I said, "Hey, Dad, what's up with you?" He told me that they were doing more tests, and he was not feeling really good. After we hugged and talked for a while, I told him I needed to go and asked whether I could pray with him.

At that moment I asked him, "Dad, do you know JESUS as your personal SAVIOR, and he looked at me with tear-filled eyes and said yes. Well, I tried to pray, but it turned into tears of joy, and all I could do was to say thank YOU, JESUS, for allowing me to know this. That was what I had been praying for—to know Dad was saved. Again the LORD answered my prayers with this divine appointment! Years later, after Dad passed away and Mom was really close to seeing Dad and JESUS, she said, "Your Dad was here last night and danced with me." I went in to see Mom, and I will never forget that moment; there was so much peace in that room.

Another divine encounter was when Mom was close to dying. Danny and I went to visit her just before she passed away. We were standing by her bed, and I said, "Mom, do you know how much JESUS loves you?" She said yes, and the whole room illuminated; it seemed as if the light from heaven came in that room and was welcoming Mom home. Danny and I both just cried with such joy in our hearts. I'm so thankful I had the honor to pray with them many times, and both told me with tears in their eyes that JESUS saved them and was LORD over their life. What glorious days those were to have that special time with each one of them. Again the LORD loves to give HIS children the desires of their heart.

Chapter 12

A Word for Timmy

THE MORNING OF FEBRUARY 8, 2003, I had set out to do a lot of appointments with clients in St. Louis, Missouri, and the LORD spoke to me to call and cancel all appointments. He told me instead to call my youngest brother and go to his home and share a word the LORD had for him. So I pulled over and called the clients and cancelled all appointments. Then I called Timmy and also called Danny to be ready to go see Timmy and his family. They lived about four hours from us at that time. Well, we made it to Timmy's and had a good time, and they so wanted us to stay overnight, but I had a message to deliver and needed to get back home. Their daughter was in school that day, so we did not get to see her, but their son was there.

The night before, the LORD had me to anoint a prayer cloth for Timmy, and HE said, "Now cut it in two and give half to Timmy to put in his wallet and the other half to his wife to pin on the pillow," so I did just that. After we talked for a while, I told them that the LORD had given me a word for Timmy. You see, Timmy was going back to Iraq for hs fourth time. He was stationed in Turkey. Timmy was in the air force. As I started to read the powerful word, which was in 1 Timothy 1:18 (KJV): "This charge I commit unto thee, son Timothy, according to the prophecies which went before on thee, that thou by them mightiest war a good warfare." This was saying to me that my brother Timothy was going to be kept safe from harm.

After reading this and speaking the words the LORD had to say, we prayed. As we stood and laid hands on Timmy, it seemed as if his whole living room lighted up and illuminated, and after the prayer, we realized it did. The presence of the LORD filled that room so full that their little son got so excited that he kept saying to us, "Wow, wow, did you see that? Did you see that?" He jumped from the floor to the couch and to another chair saying again, "Wow, wow, did you see that?" Then he said to me, "Aunt Glenda, do you have anything else in that black bag?" I said what, and he said again, "Anything else in that black bag?" Well, I realized he saw me get the Bible out of my black tote bag, and we all cried and laughed. Now think about a very young child in the middle of a prayer circle seeing the power of the LORD come down from Heaven and fill their living room, and the only way to could describe it is, "Wow, wow, did you see that!" So I want to say, always, always step into what the LORD wants you to do or where HE wants you to go, allow HIM to redirect your steps and day, for the power of the LORD will even be seen by a child!

Chapter 13

HE Heard Their Cry

I WAS WORKING LATE ONE night, and the LORD told me to "Go across the hall and lay hands on this young lady and anoint her with oil." Well, being me, I said to the LORD, "I do not know those people, and they will think I'm crazy. Besides, they are probably already gone," again being rebellious. I just kept on working, but the LORD did not lighten up. I was getting very uncomfortable, and so I stood up and took my oil and started to the door. Then I said, "Now, what if she is there; what do I say?" So again I went back to my desk and started back working. Well, all the sudden there was a knock on my door, and there stood a young lady from across the hall. She introduced herself as Vicki.

Right now I could not even tell you what she or I said, but I know what I was feeling inside, and I heard the LORD say, "I brought her to you then." My insides were feeling like I would throw up for not obeying what the LORD had told me to do, but HE is so gracious and knew this young lady needed a touch from HIM. I opened the door and said, "Come in." As we talked, I told her what the LORD had been telling me, and we both cried. She said she and her husband were going to a fertility doctor the next day, for they had been married for several years but did not have any children. Well, at that moment we started praying, and I laid hands on her and then gave her some oil that I prayed over and told her to apply it to her husband that night.

This started a wonderful friendship with the two of them, not only with us but with our son, J. W., and his family also. A few months later, Vicki told us she was expecting their first baby, and they never went to that fertility doctor. See, we knew the ONE, who created life and loves the family, had touched her that night. As it came closer the time for this baby to be born, Vicki asked me if I would go to the hospital with them and be in the delivery room with her and her husband. I said yes and that I would be honored to be there with them. When delivery time came, she called me and said they were on their way to our house for prayer and for us to go to the hospital. I was in the room with her, but then she had to have a C-section, so we prayed. Later that evening we saw their first-born son.

What a blessing that God allowed me to be a part of this, even when I was feeling so unwilling at first. Today they have three beautiful blessings, two sons and a daughter, and they love the LORD and serve HIM. I think about John 10:27 "My

sheep listen to my voice; I know them, and they follow ME."
See, Vicki also followed the direction of the LORD's voice by
coming over to my office, when the LORD told me to go to her,
which shows how, when GOD wants to touch HIS child, HE
works it out! Our family and theirs have been blessed friends
for many years. Thank YOU, LORD, for all these blessings.

Chapter 14

Blood-Stained Heart

T HE STORY BEHIND THE cover is that for several years I could feel the LORD pushing me to write about all these divine encounters. I've shared some of them with different people, some Christian and some not claiming to be, but all have had almost the same reaction. Several said it changed them, and many cried when I shared the encounters with them. Just the other day, I was in the coumadin clinic and told my nurse about this happening, and she said, "Oh my LORD, I'm having one chill after another coming through my body." She said, "I know it's the HOLY SPIRIT confirming this; hurry, and write your book. I want to buy a copy." I told her that as the years have gone by, the LORD keeps letting me feel the urge to write this book. I would say, "What will the cover be, LORD? You know I do not have one."

Since 2006, I have been in and out of the hospital with atrial fibrillation and atrial flutter several times. I have had two ablations, and now they are talking about doing a third one, so this time I felt no different. My husband said, "You need to go to the ER now," and he drove me there. When I went into the ER at Deaconess Gateway, the nurse said, "Can I help you?" When I told her I was in A-fib, she called for a wheelchair, and they took me right back to an exam room where they hooked me up to a heart monitor. The doctor came in and said my A-fib was way too fast, so he would go call my heart doctor, who is an electrophysiologist, to see what he wanted to do. This is where I had to go to be admitted to the heart hospital.

Then the RN came in the ER and said she was going start an IV to give me the medicine the doctor ordered. As she did this, she said, "Oh, I got a lot of blood on your gown, and we will change it in a minute." Well, she got busy, and I never thought anything about it. My heart doctor called and said to admit me to the heart hospital, and so they came in and moved me there. The new nurse said that they needed to put another gown on me for my heart monitor to go onto, and so she started to help me change it. When she saw the blood-stained heart, she could not speak and tears filled her eyes. One of the nurses who came in while I was changing the gown fell on her knees and said, "I just saw JESUS." She cried and cried. A lot of other nurses came in my room to see the gown, too.

At this time, I did not know my husband had taken a picture of it and stated, "We are at the ER for a heart condition to see a heart doctor. Then we were sent to the heart hospital, and this happened." Later the next day we showed it to my doctor, and he did not know what to say. We have shown it to many people, and tears always fall down their cheeks. Through the blood-stained heart on my gown from them taking my blood, the LORD told me, "Though your sins be as scarlet, they shall be white as snow" (Isaiah1:18 KJV) The blood-stained heart allowed me to witness to many nurses and doctors on how JESUS bled and died for all of us, and when they wash this gown, the blood will be washed completely away, just as JESUS died for our sins to be completely washed away. Need I say more? A few months later as I was praying, the LORD said, "There's your cover." What a witness it has been and I believe will continue to be through the writing of this book. I love the scripture Psalm 51:10 (KJV): "Create in me a clean heart, O GOD; and renew a right spirit within me."

Chapter 15

The Messenger

O N SEPTEMBER 15, 2002, I had been praying for the president of the United States to be a man after GOD'S own heart. He was on my heart almost the whole day and evening up to about midnight. I was asking the LORD all kinds of questions, mainly what can we do or how can we help him? About midnight I turned off all the lights, and I went to bed and fell fast asleep. It was 3:00 in the morning on September 16, 2002, when the LORD woke me up, and I heard Him say, "Are you ready for answers to your question and ready to write?" Years ago, the LORD told me to always have paper and pen beside me, so wherever I sit or lie down, I can be ready to write. I told the LORD many years ago, "It is okay to wake me any time!" So I got out of bed and went to my chair, turned on the light, got my Bible, paper, and pen, and the LORD said, "You have prayed, and I heard your prayers, so now be ready to write, for I'm answering you.

"Open the Bible to Deuteronomy 4, and write what I have to say to the president now." I was using the New International Version. The LORD said, "Obedience commanded," and then HE said, "Go to Deuteronomy 4:6 (NIV), and observe them carefully, for this will show your wisdom and understanding to the nations who will hear about these decrees and say, 'Surely this great nation is a wise and understanding people.' Now go to Deuteronomy 4:30–40." One thing the LORD said, was "You heard MY voice out of the fire, when the towers went down!" The LORD then said, "I do not want you to look to your right or left, but keep your eyes focused straight on JESUS, for as a president you are the commander in control, and I'm in control of this world and you."

I can remember, my hands were shaking so hard, the LORD was speaking so strong and very direct, strong but with so much love. Then to Deuteronomy 4:35 (NIV), you were shown these things so that you might know that the LORD is GOD; beside HIM there is no other! Then the LORD said; for Him to read Deuteronomy 4:39 (NIV), "Acknowledge and take to heart this day that the LORD is GOD in Heaven above and on Earth below, there is no other! And the LORD told me to get it to the president, and I said, "How am I doing this, LORD?" HE was finished; I never heard another word.

I just knew I had a mission that seemed impossible, and to tell you the truth, I felt like the president would not even listen, so all I did was cry. Then I started thinking how in the world was I going to get this to the president? I stayed up the rest of the morning and felt so drained, like all the energy had left me. I had to pack and get ready to fly out to Minnesota to do a fast-start school for a very good friend. Even this trip had been rearranged. You see, my husband was supposed to go with me, and all the sudden at the last moment changes were made, and my friend called me and said that I needed to come alone. At that time, I was not very happy about this change, but later my husband and I knew it was a GOD thing, but at that time I was a little upset.

My husband took me to the airport in Louisville, Kentucky, and at this time they did not let anyone go back with you to wait until your flight took off, so he dropped me off and went on home. I checked my bags in and went back to sit down and wait on the time to get on the plane. As I waited, I was reading, and a man came and sat His suitcase between us and said hello to me. I said, "I'm married" (why, I do not know), and he said okay, feeling uncomfortable. I got up and moved across the room to sit there, and he got up and again, came and sat right down next to me. At this point I felt the LORD leading me to say, "Do you want to know what the LORD told me to tell the president?" He said yes. I asked Him His name and what he did, and then I knew for sure it was GOD's way of saying, "Here is the messenger to deliver the papers to the president," so I shared with Him all that GOD had said and showed Him in my Bible the scripture to cover what I said.

At that point he gave me a business card, so I would know where to mail it. He was a colonel in the medical field in the army and was with the president. He said he would make sure the president received it immediately. I boarded the plane and never saw this man again. I went and taught the fast-start school and then returned home. Danny picked me up at the airport, and after we got in the car and on the road, I told Danny all about what happened. Before I left for Minnesota, I did not tell Danny anything. When we got home, I showed Danny the Bible and the writing and showed Him the business card. The next morning, Danny started typing and preparing all of this to send to the colonel. Danny later made a call to the colonel's office to let Him know that all this was on its way.

Several days later I received a letter from the president, acknowledging he received the words I sent Him that the LORD had given me for Him and a few calls from the White House to come. My husband would tease me that the CIA was going to come pick me up if I did not go to see the president, but I told Him and many others that asked me why I did not go, and I told them all, "The LORD did not tell me to go. The LORD said I was a willing vessel to be used only as the messenger to get the word to Him, so I did not go." I had prayed about going to see the president, but it was not about me and did not want the attention. This was for the president from the LORD. I did what the LORD asked, and I was released. What this taught me is that GOD works with the vessels that are willing to be used.

Chapter 16

A Sudden Call

O NE EVENING WHEN I was working in my office, the phone rang, it was our daughter-in –love. She said that she was bringing our son over to the ER, which was about a one and a half hour drive from Eldorado, Illinois, to Evansville, Indiana. She said she would drop our grandson off to us. Well, later she called back and said, "We needed to get to the ER." She went straight to the hospital due to our son being so sick. When we got to the ER, it was very noisy with a lot of people needing to be seen. Our daughter-in-love came to us and said, only one person could go back with her at a time, so I stayed in the waiting room with our grandson, and my husband went back to see our son.

Our grandson was young, and I remember thinking about how I could calm him. When he was with us and it stormed, I could sing to him, and most of the time he would fall asleep, so I started singing "There's Just Something about That Name," and sure enough he calmed right down. What I did not know until the next day is that one of the nurses in the ER came to me and said, "When you sang that song, the whole ER calmed down." It never ceases to amaze me that when the name of JESUS is spoken, all things calm down, and someone always notices it. A little while later, my husband came out and said I needed to go back with our son, and I was shocked.

He was very, very sick; he had atrial fib and was critical. We asked if he could be moved to a room. Before they moved him, we started praying, and I remember one of the nurses praying with us. When they got him into his room and we were there with him, I could feel the calming effect coming over me. We were in and out of his room that evening. His brother came in, and we prayed over him. As I laid hands on him, I heard the LORD say to me, "Tell him to open His eyes, and by his faith he was just made whole," so I said it to our son, and the LORD said, "Now leave." At this point, I felt very sick and was trying to question the LORD why. All the LORD would say is leave his room, so my husband and I left.

Our youngest son stayed overnight with his brother and said he was quite unsettled through the night. Our son's medication started working, and in a few days he was released to go home. I remember them calling us and saying he was home. A few weeks later, I saw one of the doctor's nurses. She said, "I've been with this doctor for thirteen years and have seen a lot, but, first after seeing your son so very sick, we at the hospital thought he would not make it. I was so emotional. The doctor had to send me home." She said to me again, never have I had to go home over a patient. Her eyes were so filled with tears, she said this time with joy and, tears, "What a miracle he is."

Several months went by, and I asked the LORD many times, "Why did you want me to leave our son's room?" because this took everything I had to do that. However, one day in prayer after asking the same question, the LORD said, "You will minister in many churches, and I want you to remember, when your son was small, and he asked you something, you would stoop down and look him in the eyes and say 'Right or wrong, when I say it, I will not change my mind.' Your son knew you would never lie to him or leave him being sick." Well, then the LORD said, "Tell parents to be careful about changing what they say for their child, for their life may count on it." We all saw JESUS do a mighty miracle in our son!

Our son's doctor was my heart doctor also, and at one of my appointments, he told me that he had never seen a miracle like this that happened to our son. He said, "I really did not know what to do, so I kept him on medicine for several years, but he was healed." I was able to share the LORD with him and to pray with him. It never ceases to amaze me on how GOD works. I thank GOD for our son's healing, and he still is a living testimony to it today. Praise GOD!

Chapter 17

The Prayer Cloth

ONE MORNING AS I was praying, the LORD told me to pray over a prayer cloth and send it to a dear friend of mine, Margie, who lived in Leroy, Illinois. I cut a cloth of white knit cloth and used the anointing oil I had and prayed for whatever her need was that JESUS would heal and care for her. I told JESUS, "I know how much YOU love her and want her to be well or to supply what her need may be." Later that day I mailed it with a card telling her that as I was praying, the LORD asked me to pray for her and anoint a prayer cloth and send it to her, and that she should use it as a point of contact when she received it. Several days later I received a call from this precious friend, and she said she was very, very sick with a severe headache, and her husband was getting ready to take her to the hospital. Then the mail came, he gave her the card, and she said, when she opened it, the LORD told her, "to lie down and lay it across her forehead," so she told her husband,

and she did just as the LORD told her to do. She laid the prayer cloth on her forehead and said she fell sound asleep.

She said when she woke up, she had no pain and no headache. She told me she had not slept for several days due to this sickness and the pain she had been in. She told me that, from the moment of contact from the prayer cloth, she was relieved of her headache and all sickness. She did not have to go to the hospital because the greatest Physician of all healed her. Praise GOD for HIS healing power; people should listen to that quiet, still voice, and do as HE says! I thanked the LORD for using me in such an amazing divine appointment. Read Acts 19:11–12. Pastor Bruce and his wife used to come to my office as they travel through and pray with us. Pastor Bruce would sing to us and pray, and then he would smile and say, "Just hold the ship and stand still." Now they were in their late 80s or early 90s, and they told us they go to the nursing home to minister to the old people. We would laugh and get our hugs, and away they would go to church camp. I will forever treasure these blessed memories. When I close my eyes, I can still hear him singing and the power of his prayers. These were special times with special people. Thank YOU, JESUS, for these times!

Chapter 18

Called to the Mountain

FOR MANY, MANY YEARS, in fact twice a year, spring and fall, I can hear the LORD say to me, "It's time to come to the mountain." It would make me think about Moses going up to the mountain to hear what GOD had to say; read Exodus 24:15. The feeling of the Holy Spirit was so strong that I would cry tears of hunger to go. I would tell my husband, "The LORD is calling me to the mountain," and I would make a reservation to a place outside Gatlinburg, Tennessee, to stay in a cabin way up in the mountain. One time I went into the West Virginia Mountains and sat on the side of a mountain, and the LORD would meet me there. For the five days we were there, I would get up early before the smoke would hit the mountain just at daybreak to read my Bible and pray and wait to hear HIS voice, what a fellowship we would have.

At this time, the LORD would answer so many of my prayers that I had been praying and so many questions that I had. I would write as fast as I could, and at this time, HE showed me many things in HIS word, and what it meant. HE told me how to really worship HIM in truth and love and how HE longed to speak with HIS children. After the encounter was over, I thought about the words in the Bible, "And they heard the voice of the LORD GOD, walking in the garden in the cool of the day." Read Genesis 3:8 (KJV). Some of the mornings, I would bask in HIS presence and just be still and know HE is the mighty ONE who loved me unconditionally.

You need to read Psalm 46. This is what this time reminds me of, HE says, "Be still, know that I AM GOD, I will be exalted among the nations; I will be exalted in the earth." It's my personal time with my heavenly FATHER, when I'm not a wife, mom, or grandma, just a child, and not just anyone's child but a child of the KING of KINGS, Jehovah GOD Almighty, my FATHER who wanted to be alone with me. I wanted to sit at HIS feet and be loved on by the GREAT I AM. When I was younger, it was hard to think that HE loved me so much that HE died for me and that HE wanted me to be with HIM forever and ever. I wondered what it really meant, that HE could set me free. Well I can tell you for sure, whoever the LORD sets free, is free indeed.

Since my salvation and learning by reading the word, by talking to HIM, and through all the encounters I've had with HIM, I know how much HE loves me and you. One of the greatest things is that HE willingly died to set all of us free.

My prayer is that all of you that read this book find your hiding place in HIM, steal away with JESUS, and stay there until you know just how much HE did for you and how much HE loves you. For those who do not know HIM, find HIM! The Bible says, "And ye shall seek me, and find ME, when ye shall search for ME with all your heart." Read Jeremiah 29:13 (KJV) and Jeremiah 29:14 (KJV) and be blessed!

Chapter 19

Cornfield

W E HAVE A PRECIOUS friend and his family that lives in Lynnville, Indiana. Most of his life, he has been in farming with his family—grandpa, dad, and brothers— as dairy farmers and cattle farmers. In today's world, this is a rough area to be in; prices are not always in your favor, so knowing him and his dear family for many years, it was hard to see this for them. I have seen how much of their own savings they have put back into this farm because of their love for the farm and wanting to be able to pass it down in the family to their children if all or even one of them wanted to work the farm as a living. One morning our friend called my office and told Danny he needed to talk to me, so Danny told him to come on in and that I was in the office that day. I have prayed with him and his family many times over many things concerning their lives and the things in it, so today was no different or unusual for him to call and say we need to talk and pray. He said, "I will be there in about thirty to forty minutes." He lives that far from my office, so I started praying, asking the LORD to show me just how to pray for them.

Then I got busy with some business I had to finish up. Just about an hour later, he came in the office. As we sat and talked, I could feel the HOLY SPIRIT moving me to tell him something, so I said, "This is what the HOLY SPIRIT is showing me. The HOLY SPIRIT said, 'Go out to your fields and declare a portion to the LORD before you even plant it, and all that comes from it belongs to the LORD, no matter what!'" And we prayed into this, and he went home and did exactly what the HOLY SPIRIT said! Several months went by, and we would talk and pray over the farm and his family. One day in late fall, he called my office saying he had to see me now!

Danny told him I was with someone but to come on because I would be free by the time he could get there. Danny said, "I could tell by the sound of his voice, he was excited." When he came in to the office, he had a full ear of corn in his hand and said, "In farming, usually the first two or three rows are bad due to the different things that can affect them, but the inside rows, are normally very good." He said, "This is from the first row from the field I declared for the LORD, and every row is just like this. I have never seen this happen; this is from that small piece of that field and it has yielded so much corn." He said it filled his gain bins. I wish I could give you the exact amount, but at that time I did not know I would be writing about it. I asked him if I could keep the ear of corn, and he said yes.

I took it to church on that Sunday and shared the story with the church. One of the pastors said, "I also farm and have never seen this, either. He asked if he could use the corn, and I asked him what for, and he said, "Now this will preach." For he said, as I told you, "I farm and know what he was talking about; the first few rows are normally not worth anything. They are usually bad and no good." That was one of my friend's best years of farming. So I said, "Always set aside something for the LORD ahead of time, for HE will supply." This field not only yielded an abundance of corn but also yielded a sermon that saved many.

Chapter 20

Blessed Grounds

IN THE FALL OF 2010, the LORD sent me to look at a property for us to build a new home on, so I went and then went back to the office and said to Danny, "I want to show you some property the LORD took me to, for us to build a new home," and Danny fell in love with this piece of property, too. When I went into the office to ask about this property, we found out the property we wanted was pending a sale. I found out later that it had been in a pending sale three times before we were able to get it, but GOD knew it was for us! One day at work I heard the LORD say to me to go walk the property grounds and pray over it and ask Him to bless it so that it might be a place used always for HIS service, so I did. Several weeks later, the men were to break ground for the foundation, so later that day, Danny and I went to see how they were getting along with it. As we pulled up to the property, I said to Danny, "Look at that beautiful German shepherd; I wonder which one owns him." I told Danny that I would stay in the car since there were all men standing there, but I said to him again, "Ask who that dog belongs to."

As Danny got out of the car and went up to the men where they were working, he asked them who owned the dog. I heard the men say, "We do not know, but let us tell you about this dog. He is very gentle and every time we threw a rock out of the foundation, this dog would go get it and put it back." They said this dog just wants to lie in the center of this foundation as we work. One of the men said, "We loaded this dog in our truck and took him to another property, and when we got back here, he was lying in the middle of this foundation. They could not believe it for they had taken Him far away, way out in the country, and left him there. They again loaded the dog in their truck and took off; they then went to lunch, and when they got back to our property, the dog was lying in the middle of this foundation. Again they looked at each other and said, 'How did he get back here?'" They told us that they hauled him off three times that afternoon, and each time he was back.

Well, when I heard this, I leaped out of the car and said, "You are being visited by the LORD, for you see, I prayed over this ground, and I told the LORD we would put a big rock at the corner of this house as the cornerstone, as a reminder that JESUS is the cornerstone the builders rejected!" Two of the workers started to cry and said, "I believe this." We started talking about their salvation, how great GOD is, and how much HE loves us, so we left and went back to the office. The next morning we went back to see how things were going with the building of our new home, and two of the men came and told us that as soon as the last block to the foundation was laid, they never saw the dog again. They did not even see Him leave. At that point I said, "The LORD came symbolically as a German shepherd to watch over this blessed ground for us to see HE was there all the time."

As we were talking to the men, Danny said he had taken several pictures of the foundation and the dog, but when Danny went to post the pictures, not one of the dog showed up, and Danny said, "I saw the dog in every picture I snapped, but when I posted the pictures, everything showed up, but not one showed the dog." Danny said he saw the dog, and purposely took the dog's picture many times. Again I said, "We have been visited by the LORD." Our home was finished, and we moved in June of 2011, and we have had people drive by and stop, saying they feel such a peaceful feeling as they passed our ground. Now you have to realize we live out in the country. Many people have even said, as they walked on our ground that they felt the presence of the LORD, not even knowing what happened! Yes, I believe our home is on HOLY GROUND. Thank YOU, JESUS, for allowing us to use this precious blessed place we call home, and thank YOU, JESUS, for YOUR love, protection, mercy, and grace. May we never forget how YOU restored us. May we always have a grateful heart!

Chapter 21

The Blue Hat

A VERY DEAR FRIEND OF mine said to me one day, as we were talking and sharing things that GOD has done in people's lives, "I wish you could meet my dad and mom and pray with them." I said I would love to. She later that week talked to her mom, but due to the pain her dad was in, her mom did not think her dad was up to it or that he would even want me to pray with him at this time. You know, pain changes people and how they feel and sometimes act. So we just left it alone and prayed about it. I told her, "The LORD will make the way in HIS timing." Well, her dad got really sick and ended up in the hospital, so we went to be with our precious friend as support. While there, we met her mom, brother, and sister, who were at the hospital. As I sat there, I thought, "LORD, YOU never cease to amaze me on how YOU set up divine appointments," and I truly felt this was one.

As we sat there and talked, a little later, a nurse came out of the ICU and said the family could go in to see him. We started to stay behind, and the nurse said, "You can go too," and the whole family said, "Yes, come on and see Ron." Again I should have known GOD had this planned! So we all went in, and it just so happened I was right up by Ron's head, and I asked him if I could pray for Him. He said yes. Well, that did it! We became best of friends! I mean, the bond that took place right there in that moment will always be so deep in my heart that words cannot express the love that grew out of this divine appointment.

As the months went by, we visited with both Ron and Doris, and every time Ron would be hospitalized, their daughter would call to let me know, and away we would go to see him. I always wanted Ron to know I loved him. Many times while Ron was in the hospital, I would go see him after visiting hours, so I did not take time away from his family time to be with him. I would just pop in and pray with him. Most of the time, I would take him a little something. Well, on this one day, I had planned to go see him after I went to the store. I told my husband I was ready to go to the store and then to go by and see Ron.

As I was in the store, I walked by this section and I saw a little blue sock hat. I heard the LORD say, "Buy it for Ron." I said, "But Ron has a very nice black sock hat on most of the time when I see Him; I do not think he needs this one or would even like it (imagine me telling this to the LORD, who knows all—ha-ha). Then I kind of laughed to myself. Then the LORD said it again, very loudly, "Buy it for Ron!" Now, this time I listened and picked up this little blue sock hat but still felt a little silly doing this. With this little blue sock hat in my hand, I found my husband and by the look on His face, I could tell he thought, "What now?" I told him I was ready to checkout. Again, you should have seen the look on my husband's face when he saw me carrying this little blue sock hat in my hand to the checkout.

So I said to Him, "I bet you are wondering who this is for," and he said, "That's right." I said it was for Ron, and he said, "Ron has a very nice black sock hat." I said, "I know!" I told my husband after we got into the car that the LORD told me to buy this for Ron, so that's exactly what I did. We both just kind of laughed, and I still was thinking, "Really, LORD, this hat?" Well, we got to the hospital, and when I gave Ron the hat, I wish you could have seen the smile on his face. Little did I know how special this hat would become; he loved this little blue sock hat, and he wore it all the time.

A few months later, Ron passed away, and I was honored to do his funeral. His wife said, "Oh, I forgot his little blue sock hat. I took it home to wash it, and I wanted it to go with him, but you see GOD had a different plan for this little blue sock hat." Now what happened to that little blue sock hat was the most amazing thing for me to hear. It so blessed my heart. You see, his wife gave it to Ron's sister, and she told Doris it gives her such joy to have it. She told Doris that she keeps it on the arm of her chair and said it makes her feel so close to her brother Ron still today. Thank YOU, LORD, for the small things that can mean so much! So if the LORD can use a little blue sock hat, think about how much more HE can use you!

Chapter 22

Tootsie Pops

ONE DAY I WENT to visit Ron. He was not having a very good day, so I asked him what was up with him, and he said, "I'm in a bad mood, and I have said some bad words to the nurses." I could tell he was very upset, and he said, "It's due to so much pain in my legs." His legs were extremely swollen, and when the nurses tried to move them, he would scream out in pain. He would say that they just needed to leave them alone and not touch them, but the nurses had to move them to help keep the circulation in them. He told me, "When they touch my legs, it causes me to say some not-so-nice words." You see, Ron had a change of heart, and he did not want to say cuss words anymore, but when the pain was unbearable, out they came.

So we prayed for the pain and swelling to leave and for those words to not come out of his mouth. Well, the next day I was in the grocery store, and the LORD told me to get Ron some Tootsie pops. HE said, "Get four different flavors,so I picked up a cherry, orange, chocolate, and grape." Again, you would think by this time I would just do it and shut up, but no. Again, I said, "Really, LORD? YOU want me to give Ron Tootsie pops, and for what?" Believe me, this time I really felt silly, but the LORD would not let up, so here I came with four Tootsie pops in hand. Again I wish you could have seen my husband's face, but instead of asking what they were for, he just shook his head. I smiled, thinking, "Okay, GOD, I'm doing this; no more questioned asked."

At that moment I heard the LORD say, "Tell Ron every time he gets upset and wants to say something bad, he should just pop a Tootsie pop in his mouth." Now I really chuckled inside and could feel myself smiling and saying to myself, "YOU have got this one, LORD!" So on to the hospital we went. When we got to the hospital and went into Ron's room, I said to Him, "How have you been today?" He said, "Not so good with my mouth; bad words have come out." So, out came the Tootsie pops, and I said, "From now on when you feel like the words are not going to be good, just pop it," and we laughed and laughed. Let me tell you just how great GOD is.

A few days later I went to see Ron, and when I got to his room and went in, there Ron was sucking hard on one of the Tootsie pops—the chocolate Tootsie pop. I smiled, and he smiled back. With a big grin on His face, he said to me, "I did not say anything bad; I just popped it!" Ron said this stopped the words, and he said, "I just kept sucking on this Tootsie pop," and we both laughed and laughed again. Then we prayed and thanked JESUS for the work of the Tootsie pop, for you see, a sucker can and did change the situation.

As these days have passed, I have so many blessed memories of Ron, and I thank His family for allowing me to spend time with Ron and be part of this wonderful blessing that he was. I thank the LORD for giving me time with him; he shared with me about being saved and how he loved his family! It gave me such peace to be with Ron because all the times I was not able to be with my own dad before he died, I feel like Ron filled that void. May each of you who read this always have time for someone else! The LORD hears the prayers of His children and answers them, just as HE answered Ron's daughter's prayer for me to meet her dad and mom and be able to pray with them. I am so thankful I was able to share one of Ron's daughter's favorite scriptures at his funeral, Jeremiah 29: 11, NIV: "'For I know the plans I have for you,' declares the LORD, 'plans to prosper you and not harm you, plans to give you hope and a future.'" For you see, it did just that for Ron. The plan was JESUS and hope, and a future was Heaven! Thank you, JESUS, for allowing me to be a part of this divine encounter! Every now and then, I get to spend time with the love of Ron's life, his precious wife Doris, and his daughter Tami. Sometimes I see his other children, too. Ron loved his family.

Chapter 23

Covered by the Shepherd

I WAS ASKED TO MINISTER for a women's retreat by Oak Hill Christian Center. It was to be held at Wesselman Park in Evansville, Indiana. The LORD woke me early that morning to go to the park and pray over the four corners of the shelter where we were going to be. As I was praying over the corners, moving from one corner to another, I heard something and looked up. Coming toward me from the woods was a wolf, very rough and scary-looking, and as it started to come closer to me, I lifted my hand and said, "In the name of JESUS, move on, Satan!" He stopped, looked at me, and I said it again. Then he turned and went back into the woods. In just a few minutes from that time, the ladies started showing up, and we had a great fellowship with a small breakfast.

There were a lot of ladies of all ages, ready for this word to be spoken, so I asked for prayer requests, and we stepped into HIS presence and started praying for the families represented and lifting each one up to the LORD. As I started to minister the words the LORD gave me for these women, out of the woods came a very thin, gentle German shepherd. This dog you could tell had been away from any shelter for a long time. As he came into the shelter, he sat at my feet. We tried to get him to move on, but he would not leave my feet. I gave him a drink and even tried to feed him a biscuit, but he just lay there the whole time I ministered. Later my precious daughter-in-love took a picture of this dog and put on Facebook to see if anyone was missing him, and another women said, "I will put him in my van and take him to an animal shelter," but as she was getting ready to do this, a lady drove up and said, "This is my neighbor's dog, and he's been missing for over two weeks." She said he came from way over by the zoo and that he had come from far away and had to cross many dangerous roads.

As all this was happening, I heard the LORD say, "I came to you to protect all of you; the wolf came to out of the woods," to show me symbolically that Satan will try to destroy and kill. The LORD added, "I symbolically came as a German shepherd, the ONE and only ONE, as a SHEPHERD to protect MY sheep from all harm!" The LORD said, "I showed up so you could see just how much I love you all." See, we were there ministering for broken families and bringing the children back home to the LORD, something that Satan does not want, but praise GOD for HIS showing up and His overriding protection!

It makes me think of the word in John 10:14 (NIV), "I Am the good shepherd; I know my sheep and my sheep know me."

Chapter 24

The Touch

O N FRIDAY JULY 24, 2016, at 10:00 in the morning, Danny went to get his haircut and to see if his barber was feeling better and would be able cut his hair. Danny had gone the week before and had to come back home because his barber was having chest pain and needed to go to the ER. On this morning, I told Danny I wanted to go into Evansville and run some errands, so I would go with him and sit in the car and read. I said, "Then after you're done, we can go on into Evansville." When Danny went into the barber shop, there were two gentlemen already in there, and they told Danny his barber was sick and having chest pain and that they were staying with him until his wife got there. Well, I had started reading my Bible and praying and was surprised to see Danny coming to get back in the car. I could tell he had not got a haircut.

As we were driving off, I asked why he did not get his haircut, and he said his barber was having chest pains and looked very, very sick and was waiting on his wife to come take

---

---

him to the ER. His barber has had a lot of problems with this in the past and had been in the hospital and ER quite a bit. About that time, I could hear the HOLY SPIRIT say, "Turn around and get in there," so I said to Danny, "Let's go see if he will let us pray for him." Danny turned the car around. He parked, and we went in to the barber shop. Danny asked his barber if I could lay hands on him and pray for him, and he said yes. He was calmly, sweaty, and had turned a light-gray color. I knew he was very sick and needed a touch from JESUS right then! As I started to lay hands on him, there were two other older men in there. They were waiting with him until his wife got there.

One of them said, "I'm getting in on this prayer" and stood up in front of the barber, and the other man said, "Me, too." I asked the barber if I could lay hands on him, and he said yes. I started praying; I prayed and held his hand close to his chest, and I felt the power of the LORD go through him like lightning. I could not let go of him, and I knew he had been touched and healed by the LORD Almighty. I could barely walk after this prayer because the power of the LORD coming from me into him; I felt so weak. I did not want to say anything. I was waiting to hear what the barber was going to say and about what he had felt happened.

Then one of the older men asked him how he felt and whether he felt better. The barber answered him by saying, "I sure felt something and feel okay right now," so we left. I told Danny what I had felt and knew his barber was healed. A week later, Danny went back to get his haircut and see how his barber was. His barber said, "The pain I was in at that time was extremely bad, and it stopped immediately as we prayed and has not returned!" He said he did not have to go to the ER that day and has had no pain since. For several months, Danny's barber would not let him pay for his haircuts; he told Danny, "Put your money up; it's not good in here" and he just smiled. He said after what you and your wife have done for me by praying for me, I want to do this. Danny told him, "We did it because we love you, and JESUS loves you, and HE asked us to pray for those that are sick. We obeyed HIS word; we never thought of getting any pay," and his barber said, "I know, but I want to do this for you; it's my way of saying thank you!" For those who would like to know what the Bible tells us about laying hands on the sick and they shall recover, read James 5:14. There are many more Scriptures on this. My prayer for all is to pray for others when they say they are not feeling well or are sick. Remember JESUS tells us to pray for one another. Do not walk away; someone's life may depend on it. What a privilege to pray for others.

Chapter 25

My Sister's Call

I RECEIVED A CALL FROM my youngest sister on a Sunday afternoon; she told me that she found out our brother Cliff had Stage 4 bone cancer, and at this time, he did not want to see any of us. She said she talked to him and asked him not to shut us out, that we all loved him and would do anything for him. As the days went by, I talked with my other sister and two of my brothers about calling Cliff; I knew the LORD would give me the words to say and how to pray for Cliff. Later that month my youngest sister called all of us and said she talked to Cliff, and he wanted all of us to come and spend the weekend with him. The amazing thing is, the date set was open for all five of us to go be with Cliff and His wife, Leslie. We all left on Friday to drive up to Cliff's. We all got there about three in the afternoon, so we called Cliff, and he said, "Come on now."

That night we just fellowshipped with each other and had a great meal. So Saturday we met at Cliff's for breakfast, and I felt the LORD say, "Now is the time." The LORD had been giving me the words and scripture to read and what to say. One thing the LORD had me to tell them was, "There are healings caused by medicines, there are miraculous healings, and there is eternal healing." The LORD said that we must ask JESUS into our hearts and forgive ourselves and others. So before I laid hands on him, the first thing was to ask the LORD to forgive each one of us and anyone whom we held anything against and to accept JESUS into our hearts so that we would have a clear, clean heart. The word says in James 5:16 (KJV), "Confess your faults one to another, and pray one for another, that ye may be healed. The effectual fervent prayers of a righteous man availeth much."

We had such an amazing time praying; the power of the LORD was all over each one of us. After the prayer, some of them went outside, and above them were contrails from two planes that had crossed over, and we saw a mighty cross. Then they looked, and on His home was a praying mantis. Some of my brothers and sisters were praising the LORD over those signs. On Sunday, we all went to breakfast and then went to Starved Rock, for my brother Cliff built the welcome center there and the power plant across the river. They were amazing. After that we all went home.

A few weeks later, we got a call to come to Peoria, Illinois, that Cliff had become very, very sick. He had new symptoms that did not match any of the cancer he had. When we got to the Peoria hospital, Cliff was in the ICU. He was totally unable to move any part of His body and had become totally blind. This lasted for forty-eight days. All the doctors were totally stumped, so I prayed and spoke life into Him. He said something was pulling Him down into a deep dark hole, and I said, "We are children of light, and JESUS is pulling you into light. JESUS and I refuse to let you go!"

One morning praying over Cliff, I felt the LORD saying he needs His blood flushed and cleansed, so I told Cliff and His wife and all my sisters and brothers. Then I told the LORD that a doctor had to be able to tell us what is wrong with Cliff. He was getting worse as the days went on. Just a day later, a doctor came into Cliff's room and in twelve minutes knew what was wrong with Him. This doctor ordered the blood test and a plan of action. He gave us a name, Miller Fisher syndrome. We stayed the night, and I came home early the next morning. The LORD woke me up and told me to get on the computer, and HE took me to a site that told all about this disease, and there it was as bold as can be: to do a plasmapheresis to cleanse His blood. I copied it all and highlighted it.

Then I called Cliff's wife Leslie and said I was going to overnight this all to her and to please give it to Cliff's Dr. H., for there is a special blood test to tell if Miller Fisher syndrome is still in Cliff's body. Dr. H.'s office is in Peoria. Several days later when I was at the hospital, this doctor came in Cliff's room. He said just what I had said about needing to flush and cleanse Cliff's blood. Leslie said to this doctor that's what his sister has said all along and that the LORD told her. The doctor said that this is not how you really say it that way to flush and cleanse the blood; he knew and we knew it was JESUS confirming that this is the right diagnosis, and this doctor already had it all set up to do. After Cliff had the plasmapheresis done, he was able to go home. They had many family members to help Him and Leslie out, and I was blessed to stay two weeks with Him. Cliff still has a very rough road to walk; His eyesight has been restored, and he is walking without a walker.

I returned to Cliff's on Easter Sunday because he had chemo on Tuesday, the sixteenth; it was supposed to be a very strong and rough chemo, and he and his wife wanted me there. I had the prayer chain in our church and all church family and friends and all our brothers and sisters praying for the LORD to intervene if Cliff was not strong enough to get this chemo at this time, for he was so very, very weak, and we could see that he could not go through that right now. This is what happened, and GOD did just that! Earlier the LORD had given me a word for all my brothers and sisters to pray over Cliff. It was Isaiah 54:17. The LORD said to pray over all medicine and chemo drugs and say, "No weapon formed against Cliff will prosper, no chemo and no medicine," so we prayed this almost around the clock.

On Sunday night about seven in the evening, my husband said good-bye to Cliff, for he was going to our home in Indiana, and all of a sudden, Cliff got to feeling really bad and could not sit up. Leslie took Him back to their bed to go to sleep. Casper, a good friend of Cliff's, came Monday morning to take Cliff to get His blood test done at the cancer center. Well, in about thirty-five minutes, Casper came back without Cliff, and he said Cliff was having to get an IV for magnesium because he had passed out, and he would go back and get Him in a couple of hours. When Casper went to get Cliff, he passed out again, and they told Him to take Him straight to the ER and from there, the doctor in the ER said, "I'm sending Cliff by ambulance to OSF hospital in Peoria, Illinois." So Cliff did not start chemo.

We know the LORD intervened and answered our prayers to stop the chemo until Cliff could get stronger. Cliff's sister-in-law Kathy said, "This sure caused me to believe!" When they got Cliff in an ICU room, he passed out again, and all his doctors were there. Dr. Lisa started getting things done for Cliff, ordering all kinds of tests. The first test was an EKG, and the man who came in to do it said, "I feel the presence of the LORD." I said we have the same FATHER, and he clapped His hands and said, "That's what I'm talking about!" Later he came and gave me a card. It said "Pastor Brown."

The next day, Cliff was moved to another room on the ICU floor, and the RN who was assigned to Cliff came into His room while I was quoting scripture to Cliff. This RN quoted it right along with me. RN Jason, what a powerful man of GOD; he shared His testimony with Cliff and was there all day. When His shift was over and he started to go home, the LORD directed Him back to Cliff's room for prayer. We both agreed that this was a divine appointment for Cliff. So far, through all these days, I had many ask about this JESUS and wanted to know HIM, and I saw a very good friend of Cliff's saved and many more GOD events.

One morning the LORD woke me up at 3:33 a.m. and told me to go to Jeremiah 33:3, and I said, "Okay, LORD, but I know that by heart." The LORD said read on to Jeremiah 33:6 (KJV), "Behold, I will bring (Cliff) it health and cure, and I will cure (Cliff) them, and reveal unto (Cliff) them the abundance of peace and truth." He said this was for Cliff. Now that day I told Cliff and Leslie, and then I read the word to them. Around two hours later, Cliff was a code blue, and Leslie was out in the hall calling on the LORD, saying, "Please, GOD, not this way!" That next morning, the LORD woke Leslie up at 3:33 a.m., and she sat straight up in the bed and stared at the clock. She later told me about it, and I heard the LORD say, "I heard her call and cry and answered her."

I gave Leslie confirmation by the clock, to remind her about Jeremiah 33:3. I had all of the family praying that if Cliff was not strong enough, for GOD to intervene and stop the chemo, and GOD did just that! Later one of the doctors who was in the room with Cliff looked me in the face and said, "You got your confirmation from GOD!" Now you have to understand this doctor knew nothing, and I do not believe he even knew what he was saying to me, but GOD confirmed HIS words once again to all of us! The LORD has supplied so many other great things and words. Well, Cliff got home, and I was home for a few days. We met with the cancer doctor, and he wanted to do this chemo on May 16, and I went back with Cliff and Leslie for this to be done, reading the word over Cliff and praying in the HOLY SPIRIT for GOD will to be done here on earth as in heaven, right now.

Cliff has had four chemo treatments and is doing well. I laid hands on Cliff and a prayer cloth with anointed oil and pinned it to his tee-shirt on May 23, 2017. I'm home, and our youngest sister, Tonnie, is with him, and she has been using the oils on his back, chest, and legs to detox his body. I believe her touch is anointed by JESUS. Tonnie and Kathy took Cliff to have a lifetime port put in and Cliff had a lot of swelling in his body. One nurse practitioner was afraid of kidney failure due to swelling and not urinating enough, so they ordered more blood tests, and Cliff was very afraid. Again the LORD gave me a word, so I called Tonnie and read it and then prayed. A few hours later, my sister called and said Cliff had just talked to the doctor and they said, "Your tests are better than they have been in a very long time; just stay the course."

Our younger brother, Timmy, and his wife will be there with them on Monday June 5, and then I will be going back to stay with Cliff again on June 9 unless he does not need me, and that would mean he is up caring for himself, and we would shout the victory! GOD has been faithful in Cliff's life; we keep on walking by faith and praying with him for a total healing.

There are so many other things that have happened along this journey that it is very hard to tell it all, but we know GOD has HIS hands on Cliff and has given Cliff favor by going ahead of all this, finding the right doctors to be on Cliff's case. I believe it was easier for the LORD to work through animals and then through humans, for it seems we all have our own thoughts and ways, not realizing HE needs us to help and listen to HIM. HE is such a gentleman that HE will not go against your will; HE will gently nudge you. My pray is for all to find HIS will for your life, for it is the best thing that can ever happen to you and allow JESUS to work through you. So never give up praying for others; you may be on the brink of that miracle.

Chapter 26

Confirmation

THE DAY I FINALLY knew it was time to put all these divine encounters together, I started pulling out all the little notes from many of my Bibles and in journal books that I have written down over the years and kept for such a time as this. The next day, Danny and I started praying over which publisher to use, for I did not want one that would try to change the wording of these divine encounters, for these are true and the truth is spoken in them. The next morning I knew the company that I would go with, so I told Danny, and we prayed into this company. The next day I chose to go with Xulon Press. I called and left a message for Chris S. to please call me, and he did. We talked and discussed all the packages, and I felt that he was great help and only wanted the best for me, so I told him I would talk to my husband and pray over it and call him back later. Well, I called him, and we started the process, which was great.

Now this really gets better, for you see, the next morning I opened my laptop up to Facebook, and there stood Chris S. in a picture with our Pastor Jay and both their families in Florida. I found out that they have been friends and in the ministry serving together for years, and also Pastor Jay served with Chris's Dad in the ministry. Well, do I need to say this was a big wow moment for us? I turned the laptop around and said to my husband, "You are not going to believe this one!" We both knew it was an answer from the LORD saying, "You chose the right company!" And to top this off, our pastor's wife, Kim, came to me before church started and said, "You know that Jennifer, Pastor Mike's wife has a sister who is married to Chris's brother." So do you see why I know that HE will direct your steps? When I talked to Chris and asked Him if he was with our Pastor Jay, he said, "What, your pastor?" Then he said, "I believe this is a divine appointment." Chris S. later told me he talked to Pastor Jay and said, "How can it be, one of your members is doing her book with our company, and you know her very well." Only GOD can, so go, GOD!

Chapter 27

Anointed

I N AUGUST OF 1982, I was praying and asked the LORD to anoint me for the service of children. Our sons would have been ten and seven. I really felt that call on my life. One evening we were at a ballgame in Eldorado at the grade school. Our oldest son's team was playing that night, and I was really ready to enjoy watching His game. Just as it started, one of our friends pulled up to watch their son play, and they had a little baby girl with them; one of their family's little one they were taking care of, and she was screaming and crying. The aunt said she has been crying a lot, missing her mommy.

Well, after a short time of them trying to calm her down, I asked if I could help by holding her. The aunt said, "You can try, but she normally won't let anyone strange hold her at all," so I took her and immediately she hushed and fell sound asleep as I whispered the precious name of JESUS in her ear. The peace that came over that little girl was amazing. Everyone around us noticed the hush and was talking about my touching her and how quickly she calmed down, so I shared the calling I felt, and the proof was right in front of us that JESUS had blessed me and anointed my touch. This little girl slept on my lap through both games. The aunt told me days later at another ball game that the little girl stayed calm and played and was so good.

That was the peace that only GOD can give. The Word says, "and the peace of GOD, which passeth all understanding, shall keep your hearts and minds through CHRIST JESUS" (Philippians 4:7 KJV). This has happened many different times in my life and in many different places we have been, even in the grocery store when little ones acted up, and the parents were beside themselves. One time, a mother came to me and asked me to let her little one take naps at my house because her newborn would not sleep for her. She was a new mom and a very nervous one, and the baby felt it; it also was a way the LORD allowed me to minister to his mommy, and she was saved. So ask GOD to anoint you in HIS service and to use you, and HE will, if it's from your heart.

Chapter 28

Never the End

THIS IS NOT THE end; there will be more and more divine encounters with the LORD as the days go on until we hear the trumpet sound, and then may we say, "even so LORD JESUS come." May you all start to recognize the call on your life and step into HIS presence and move as HE wants you too. Remember the word says in Matthew 22:14 (KJV), "For many are called, but few are chosen." If I say it in my own words, few will answer the call, so let it come from the **SPIRIT** of GOD! May you all read Isaiah 6:8 (KJV). Also I heard the voice of the LORD saying, "Whom shall I send, and who will go for us?" Then I said, "Here am I, send me!" Stir the flame of YOUR fire in me, JESUS; may we all ask the LORD, "What can I do for YOU?" People need to act to HIS voice; those who have ears hear what the LORD is saying!

Sixty-Two Days of Food
for Thought

THESE ARE THOUGHTS THAT the LORD gives me daily, and I pray they encourage you.

1. Food for Thought: We know there is power in prayer, and there is power when you're in His presence, so I choose to stay in HIS presence. I want to feel HIS love, I want to know HE is there all the time, and I want to live for HIM. HIS way is always the best way for me and my family's life! So run to HIM and stay in HIS presence, for you will receive peace, love, comfort, and most of all, mercy and grace! There is no better place than to steal away with JESUS and stay until all your burdens are taken away. Now smile for the *Son*shine is covering you, and have a blessed day.

2. Food for Thought: This is the time of the year for new things to be seen every day, so be sure you look around everywhere you go. Now is the time to slow down and watch the

beauty of the LORD unfold; some flowers only bloom for a few days, and I do not want to miss them. This causes me to realize just how precious life is. It is here today and gone tomorrow. As a child I always thought my mom and dad would live forever, and now it seems as they have been gone forever. May you take one day at a time and enjoy the time you are in; remember to thank JESUS for all HE has done for you, what HE has supplied you with, and for healings of your body, mind, and soul. Now it's time to share HIM and HIS love with others, and remember to smile, for JESUS loves you, this I know. Allow your smile to be used by JESUS so that it might shine on someone else today. Have a blessed day.

3. Food for Thought: Who remembers the saying, "Stick and stones can break my bones, but words can never hurt me." Well, we know how wrong this is: "Words can never hurt." We know words stay with a person forever; most likely, words are never healed. So my prayer for all of us is to use words that are lifting others up, encouraging, and most of all, words that will cause people to want to remember them forever. Be a word planter of blessings to everyone you know and a seed planter of love and joy. It takes the same amount of time to sow good or bad words. JESUS, I ask forgiveness for ever hurting anyone with a word. May

the blessings of the LORD cover each one of us and show us how to forgive.

4. Food for Thought: Every day we get up, and we pretty much do the same things; we are pretty much set in our own ways. The thing I love so much is every day with JESUS is sweeter than the day before. My prayer for all is to spend more time with JESUS, praying for others, and then each day will be different. People need to know they are prayed for. May the blessings from the LORD who blesses us and covers us all daily, always be with you. So open up your heart and let the LORD in.

5. Food for Thought: It's funny that I would think about fishing when I do not and never have been fond of fishing, but I had a dad and have a husband and sons and a grandson who love it. This morning as I was thinking about fishing, the LORD said, "Fishermen use depth finders to find out where the fish are and see the fish that go down deep and some even stay in a school." I said, "Yes, I know that from hearing them all talk about their fishing trips." The LORD said to me, "I Am the true depth finder; you can never go too deep for me not to find you, and when I find you, I will throw you a lifeline and will rescue you out of the deepest waters of life." So remember the true depth finder has HIS

fishermen out looking all the time for you, and HE will bring you and your life into shallow waters where you can stand again. So shout, for JESUS came to save, and a lifeboat is on your way. Amen.

6. Food for Thought: We as Christians, which means CHRIST-like, need to stand for right, even if all the world around us wants us to conform to it, for we have a blessed book that teaches us the right way. The LORD says that HE will direct our path, and HE will show us the right way; remember it's easy to live the worldly way. So I ask all Christians to stand firm and pray for HIS will to be done, here on earth as is in heaven, right now. Remember when we are weak, HE is strong; remember you will be rewarded for doing right, even when the world does not see it that way. So my prayer this morning for all is to stand in agreement with this precious book, the Bible, believe every word in it, and allow the LORD to be the leader of your life. Where HE leads, we will follow; may our prayers be heard in heaven, and may the healing on this earth begin. May all see the good in his or her fellow man and stop judging, may we show HIS love and caring for others, and may HIS will be done in your life. So think on the LORD and HIS ways all the days of your life, for there is no better way than HIS; smile and share the LORD with someone today.

7. Food for Thought: As I looked out the window this morning, I see light blue with pink in the sky, and then I looked at the lake and watched the water ripple. Then I noticed the birds in the grass looking for something for something to eat; there are bluebirds, purple martins, tree sparrows, robins, and black birds. What I want you to see in this is the beauty of this world that I'm describing to you. Do you take time to see the natural beauty before you? What you see can cause a calming to come over you from the inside out; there is power in color and life. I try to enjoy every season for what it is: winter is a season of rest for the ground, and spring a season of new life all around us. It makes me think about the LORD. HE says come to me, and I will give you rest, HE restores us when we are weak, and most of all, HE gives us hope and a life that we will live forever with HIM as long as we have called upon HIM to save us. Therefore, right now, ask HIM into your heart. JESUS, forgive our sins and come into my heart as our SAVIOR. Amen. Now smile and share HIS love with others.

8. Food for Thought: There are a lot of people today and in the past who are known for their works But I was reminded that JESUS loves and cares for us for who we are, not what we do; yes HE wants us to work in the kingdom, but HE wants more for us to belong to HIM and be HIS child.

My prayer is for you to really get to know the FATHER and HIS unconditional love for you and to know HIS arm is not shortened but outstretched. Oh, how HE loves you and me. Step into HIS presence, allow HIM to hold you, and tell others that HE waits to hear their voice. Now smile and share HIS love with others.

9. Food for Thought: Take a deep breath and realize that JESUS loves you just as you are. HE will make a way for you, so your part is to listen and be ready to answer and say yes when HE knocks on your heart's door. The best way to get to know HIM is to get grounded in HIS word in the Bible. Get in a Bible-teaching church, and learn to serve, to walk daily in HIS light, and allow HIM to flood you with HIS love, peace, and joy, for HE gives HIS mercy and grace to make a way for you. So get up, get in church, and then go expecting something amazing to happen. Let it start in you, and then share it with others and choose to have a blessed day.

10. Food for Thought: Today is a new day; it's time to get up and start a prayer list. Start your day off praying for others. When you move in this direction, you begin to feel up lifted and see your problems as not bad; the atmosphere changes in your spirit. People need our prayers; this world has nothing to offer them but pain, sickness, and disappointment. We

can shed light in their darkness, so make it a point daily to lift others in prayer. There are really no words that can describe just how deep the love JESUS has for your family and friends; it's unconditional, for HIS hands are unchanging and are huge to hold all of us at one time. What a privilege to carry everything to HIM in prayer. Allow the SON to shine in you, and share it with someone today.

11. Food for Thought: It always amazes me that there is so much healing in the truth. The word says, "Then you will know the truth, and the truth will set you free" (John 8:32 NIV). Get deep into HIS word and seek HIS peace that passes all understanding and then stand and wait on HIM. Do not keep HIM to yourself; share your story of what HE has done for you and how HE loves all of us. Thank HIM for giving you this peace and love, and then live free from all harm, wrapped in HIS loving arms. Share this with someone today.

12. Food for Thought: How well do we really listen? Every minute of the day, the LORD speaks to HIS children in some form; the best way to hear from HIM is to read HIS word. Have you ever felt led to pray for someone or go see someone or take food to someone? Who do you think tells you that? Well, I know all good things come from the

LORD. Also, if you're HIS child, the word tells us we know HIS voice and HE knows yours. My prayer for all of us is to have a listening ear and then to go do as it has said. May we not miss HIS call on our life or for someone else. Use us, LORD JESUS. Amen.

13. Food for Thought: You know you love it when someone says thank you for your caring or for a kind word or deed you may have done. Everyone wants to hear praise for what they have done; just a thank you can change your day. Well, JESUS loves to hear you say thank YOU for all the blessings, love, peace, and joy that HE gives to us daily, so please stop and count your blessings. My prayer for all us is to stop and be still and start praising and thanking JESUS for your life, family, church, friends, health, supplying your needs, and giving you your wants. There is healing power in being thankful, in JESUS name. Amen.

14. Food for Thought: This morning after reading the word and praying and thinking about the day ahead of me, I could hear the words "Stand by ME." Wow, the LORD, who loves me so much, is telling me to stand by HIM in all the days of my life no matter what the day brings! So this tells me, HE is with me all the time, HE will never leave me, and that we are so close that we are inseparable! This is a reminder

that HE will never leave me, so the question is, do you or I leave HIM out until there is such a need, all we can cry out and say, "Where are you, JESUS? or "Where have YOU been?" Then HE calmly says, "I never walked away. I'VE been here all the time. It was you who moved away." So my prayer for all is to bow the knee right now and say, "Here I am, JESUS, and here I will stay. I will stand by YOU forever." Amen.

15. Food for Thought: As I got up this morning and stepped outside facing the bright sun and feeling the chill in the air, it caused me to think of the song "Joy Comes in the Morning." It caused such a peace and filled me with HIS joy, for light had come after a dark night. Each one of us needs to give ourselves time for each moment and to reflect on it. Just think how the sun can warm your body and feed it vitamin D for healing to make you feel happy. Well, I know a ONE who warms me and fills me with true joy and will never fade away; it is the SON of GOD, JESUS. My prayer for all is to open up your heart and allow this SON to come in and give you joy, unspeakable and full of His glory, so take time to rest and reflect. Do not hurry the daylight away, as they say, stop and smell the roses, and pray that you will find this kind of time in your life, in JESUS name. Amen.

16. Food for Thought: Where do I start this morning? The LORD has shown me so many things; first HE said, "Be still and know that I AM GOD" (Psalm 46:10–11; KJV). HE said, "I will be exalted!" My prayer for all is to listen and obey; just listen and be still. Those that have ears hear what the word of the LORD is saying. JESUS loves you for who you are! Press into HIM, for HE waits to hear your voice and your praise. Amen.

17. Food for Thought: Every day I raise my hands and praise the LORD for all HIS blessings. HE is an amazing FATHER who loves all HIS children so very much. As the storms of life roll and the rain falls, just take the time to thank HIM for the new season we are entering—new life, and new color. Pray that the LORD will keep us safe from the storms of the weather and the storms in your life. Remember there is power in the name of JESUS, and even the wind and rain have to obey HIS voice. Therefore, call out to HIM today. Take time and ask HIM to breathe in you and thank HIM for each day, and put your life in HIS care, for HE loves you. Do not worry about tomorrow, for tomorrow will worry about itself. Read Matthew 6:34 (NIV).

18. Food for Thought: Watching all the birds around our home this morning as they busy themselves choosing their

nesting box or the right martin house, and watching them busy at gathering all the material to build their nest, it made me realize how personal they made their nest and did not want any other bird in it. It caused me to think about the word in Matthew 6:26–34. You need to read this. It tells me if GOD so loved the sparrows, I know HE loves me more. It tells me HIS eye is on the sparrow, and we are far more valuable than them; it tells me not one of them falls to the ground without HIM knowing it. So I thank YOU, JESUS, that we are so loved and that we cannot fall without YOU catching us and knowing right where we are. Call on the LORD, and ask HIM what HIS will for your life is, and then be still and listen. Read Jeremiah 29:11 NIV— "For I know the plans I have for you, to prosper, give you hope and a future." Wow, now that's amazing, but HE is an amazing GOD.

19. Food for Thought: Have you ever thought about just how much GOD really cares for you? Did you know that HIS love extends way down deep in your soul and way beyond the grave? Did you know the HE wants us to keep HIS commandments? One blessing I love is in Revelation 22:14 KJV that says, "Blessed are they that do HIS commandments that they may have right to the tree of life, and may enter in through the gates into the city." Praise the

LORD for HE is good. Now is the time to answer the question and thank HIM for HIS mercy and grace.

20. Food for Thought: Are you like me and have to make a shopping list, important things to-do list, and an appointment list? Ha-ha. But did you know the most important list there is, is a prayer list? Now if you make a prayer list, add me to it; my needs are family, church family, and friends. Become a prayer partner to someone, and pray with them, for there is power in prayer. I believe in prayer you can move the mountain, for the prayer of the righteous are heard. James 5:16 KJV says it this way: "Confess your faults one to another, and pray one for another, that ye may be healed. The effectual fervent prayer of a righteous man availeth much." So pray, my precious friends, and listen for HIS answers.

21. Food for Thought: As I was worshiping and praying, these words came to me. We sing of power, we sing of love, and we sing of the anointing from the FATHER above, so move into HIS anointing, and be covered with HIS power and love. So sing of these gifts given to you from your Heavenly FATHER above. Now praise HIM and worship HIM in truth and spirit. Amen.

22. Food for Thought: Early this morning just before daybreak, I was getting my coffee when I noticed the sky. I actually said *wow;* it was still pretty dark, and all of a sudden, a line of white came down from the heavens; not lightning, it was like the sky parted in two. I thought, this is how the eastern skies will be split at the sound of the trumpet, as the word says Matthew 24:27 KJV, "For as the lightning cometh out of the east, and shineth even unto the west; so shall also the coming of the SON of man be." Everyday look up to JESUS, for HE is the only one who can save you and qualify you to have eternal life.

23. Food for Thought: Did you know that the LORD knows the stars by name? What great news this is for us. You see, you are HIS pride and joy, and everything in this world was made for HIS children to enjoy. We are greater than any star could ever be. HE knows you by name. The word says HE knew you before you were formed. Just read Jeremiah 1:5; this should tell you just how much HE loves you, and I so thank HIM today for all HE has done for you.

24. Food for Thought: When you get up, give thanks, and as the day goes on, give thanks; learn to praise the LORD with everything in you. When you start to feel down, think about someone else, start praying for them, and watch

your thoughts turn to good and your feelings start to be lifted up. When things seem bad and you really do not know what to do, just say, "My JESUS is bigger than how I feel or anything I may go through. He is bigger than any mountain and bigger than any sickness," and ask JESUS to answer all doors in your life and to walk before in them. Now smile, for the LORD loves you and will shine through you, so let go and let GOD be in control.

25. Food for Thought: We know the saying goes "April showers bring May flowers," so that means we have to go through more weather changes, but one thing I know for sure, in the ever-changing circumstances of life, there is a faithful, never-changing GOD in control of my life. HE is the only ONE who could say, "JESUS CHRIST the same yesterday, and today and forever" (Hebrews 13:8 KJV), so you can count on HIM!

26. Food for Thought: Every day I look to the LORD for my needs, and I know the song that I sang when I was younger still stands: "I can even walk without YOU holding my hand, each day has so many of its own troubles, there is always a decisions to make and I know HE knows the best for our life." So call on the LORD for all your needs, then be still and allow HIM to answer. Many times HE will answer

you in a thought or another person or reading HIS word. Praise HIS powerful name for all HE did, when HE walked on earth, HE can still and will do. Remember it's our faith and believing in HIS word that can move the mountain. Smile, for JESUS loves you, this I know. Be blessed and be a blessing to someone today.

27. Food for Thought: It was a rainy day outside. The wind howled, and the sky was dark, but I was singing with a smile on my face because I know the maker of the wind, and I know the maker of the rain. HE calms the storm and tells the sun to shine again, for I know the maker of the wind! This season gives the earth the drink it needs and so I'm thankful for liquid sunshine. So let the sunshine in, face it with a grin, and choose to have a blessed day.

28. Food for Thought: This morning I woke up, with a song on my mind; I sang it and cried and prayed and worshiped the LORD . My prayer is, if you wake up or just hear a song in your mind sing it out loud and worship JESUS with it. For it will bless you and cause your day to be brighter. Praise causes you to release troubles, Amen

29. Food for Thought: Have you ever thought about a bridge, and what it is for? We know it connects one side to another.

It may be the only way for you to get from one place to many other places, and there may be many bridges that you have to cross before you reach your final trip. I believe faith and believing are bridges in our life. I think they are the bridge to GOD! I think they are the bridge to where I am and the place to where GOD wants me to get to. You may cross many bridges before you get to the place GOD wants you, but push forward and hold on to your faith and believe HE is able to see you through. JESUS, thank YOU for all my bridges, so move me to that place, that secret place in YOU!

30. Food for Thought: Praying this morning and thinking about words and thoughts caused me to read Psalm 100:4 (KJV) to enter into HIS gates with thanksgiving and into HIS courts with praise, being thankful unto HIM and blessing HIS name. The word thanksgiving makes me stop and be thankful for everything small and big, even to be thankful for the moment. JESUS is in the good times and the rough times, so all the time praise the LORD. Now line up your thoughts and words with how you have been praying, and you soon will see a breakthrough; always be filled with gratitude towards JESUS, and be thankful for one day at a time.

31. Food for Thought: If you're like me, you love to relax and reflect. I love to sit and think about how the day went,

and what is planned for tomorrow. Some times when I'm reflecting on the day, I catch myself smiling. I know how the LORD wants us to rest in HIM and to think good thoughts. I realize HE is the only way I make it through every day, and I feel the peace that only HE can give. My prayer for all today is to rest in HIM, lay it all down, and receive all HE has for you; be still and listen well, for HE speaks in many ways to HIS children. One way I can count on hearing HIM is to pick up HIS word, the Bible, and read and pray. So dive into the Bible with both feet now.

32. Food for Thought: Thinking about what can I do, and this comes to my mind, being a servant. Now I thought there are many ways to serve, and the LORD loves for us to serve others. HE came to serve, not to be served (Matthew 20:28 NIV), and see what that says to you, for to me it's a big wow. The KING of kings came to serve, and HE calls us to serve others. My prayer is for each one to ask the LORD, "How I can start serving today?" and if you already do, for the LORD to increase your territory in this field. Amen.

33. Food for Thought: Words have power; try using words like favor of the LORD and the blessing of the LORD to cover you. Try speaking words of encouragement over your family and friends as you pray for them. Call someone

and use words to lift them up; let them know you pray for them, and find out what their needs are. Then move into the direction to be a helping hand. I often hear someone tell a joke that they think is funny but not very clean in words, and then they wonder why their children tell some not-so-funny, dirty jokes. Words can really break us, so stop and think before you say a word, which cannot be taken back.

34. Food for Thought: Thinking about how people try to figure out what will happen tomorrow or even next week is not wise; we should not be too worried about what is coming. We need to learn to trust in JESUS, for HE supplies our every need. Remember HE tells us HE holds our life in HIS hands and has a plan for us. I sometimes try to act like I have a better plan and find myself in a big mess, and HE comes to my rescue. Have you ever been there? My prayer for all is to trust and obey! Trust the LORD with all our heart, and stop worrying because HE has this.

35. Food for Thought: This morning may you seek the LORD with all your heart; ask HIM for wisdom, knowledge, and understanding. Take a closer walk with HIM, remember, just one day at a time. May you diligently seek divine wisdom and let HIS words fill your heart, mind, and soul. Ask HIM to allow you to walk in discernment. Ask the LORD

to show you the area of weakness in you so that you can pray for strength to do HIS will for your life. May you pick up your Bible and read and memorize HIS word, so it can be hid in your heart forever.

36. Food for Thought: I was thinking today about the name of JESUS, and a question came up in my mind about healings. I could hear JESUS say, "Do you believe I was raised from the dead?" I said, "Yes, I know YOU were." Then he said, "When you speak MY name, do you believe I can do the same today as yesterday and tomorrow?" Wow, this was such an amazing moment; it caused me to repent for using the name of JESUS without totally believing HE can. Right now HE can! So my prayer for all is to know when you use the name of JESUS, whatever has been will be again. Amen.

37. Food for Thought of the Day: Today is the day for you to become a sower, not for money, but for souls to be saved. Ask the LORD to put someone on your heart, and pray for that person until there is a breakthrough; send them cards, call them, and lift them up. Find out if there is a need, and pray that the LORD will help you meet it for them; it's amazing what JESUS will do if you ask.

38. Food for Thought: Thinking about words and the power they have, ask the LORD to help you choose the words you use daily as pleasing to HIM. I love to use words that lift people up and at the same time lift me up also. Try using "blessings of the LORD," "favor of the LORD," "have a blessed day." Think about how damaging words are and how they hurt or think about how encouraging they can be. Which would you rather hear from someone else or even hear out of your mouth? So thank YOU, JESUS, for precious words of love.

39. Food for Thought: I think about JESUS and HIS name and the power when we speak HIS name. HE is the same today as yesterday and will be tomorrow. Everything in the Bible is the word of truth, and with that said, you can pray and believe that what has ever been written. All promises and all benefits belong to HIS children, and if HE ever healed someone, HE still heals today, so grab ahold of HIS name and believe when you call on HIS name!

40. Food for Thought: I have been thinking today about the HOLY SPIRIT and how HE will guide you and allow you to know what to do and where to go, so today I ask you to just sit still and ask the HOLY SPIRIT to make Himself known to you. Just sit there and receive what the LORD has for you, and never let go of HIS presence that is covering you

right now. Press into HIM and know you never have to fear, for HE is with you right now through it all. HE will never let go of you, so sing praise to HIM.

41. Food for Thought: What do you look for in a friend? Do you know the Bible says that a friend will stick to you closer than a brother? When I look for a friend, I look for someone who will accept me for who I am, someone who will lift me in prayer and ask, "Can I be a helping hand?" I look for someone who does not talk badly about others, and one who laughs with me and cries with me. Well, I found a friend in JESUS; HE hugs me, accepts me just as I am, HE's never too busy for me, HE listens, and has my back all the time. How would you like a friend like this JESUS? Would you love to meet JESUS? You can, right there were you are; just ask JESUS to forgive your sins and come into your life forever and be your SAVIOR and friend. HE will right now!

42. Food for Thought: Come, LORD JESUS, into my heart. I'm so hungry for you, and I want to be close to you. I want to feel your heart beat with mine. I want to drink from YOUR fountain that never will run dry; I want YOU as my comforter, my strong tower, and my resting place. Help me to look to YOU for everything and come to YOU before I try the world's way. Keep me under YOUR wings, FATHER GOD. Amen.

43. Food for Thought: Let this be the day you think on the things that are really important to you. Try to think about how they affect you daily and how blessed you are to be who you are! I first try to think about how blessed I am to be chosen by the LORD to be one of HIS children and how HE gave me the heart to make the right choices and be the person I am, for HE is still working on me. JESUS molds us and makes us every moment of the day, and HE has a great design for your life. Step into HIS presence, allow yourself to seek HIS face, and just take the time to linger with HIM. All the things of this world will grow strangely dim for the light of HIS mercy and grace over your life. Ask JESUS to show you HIS ways. Amen.

44. Food for Thought: What do you think happens when you have the heart of JESUS? You begin to see things differently and you start to see with eyes of compassion, eyes full of true love. You hear a small voice cry for help and see beyond the makeup to see others for whom they really are. You soon begin to feel the hurt of someone who says it's okay but is really broken inside and needs someone to say, "Hold on for the morning is coming; just ride out the storm, and I will ride it with you." Oh to have the heart of JESUS should be what we all are crying for, so help us, JESUS, to be more like YOU. Amen.

45. Food for Thought: Have you ever heard a person say its all okay, but they are dying inside? Have you ever asked JESUS to allow you to have unconditional love for others? Have you ever asked JESUS to allow you to share HIM with someone and to be bold but not rude? Have you ever asked JESUS to help pick up the cross and follow HIM? Are you willing to follow HIM no matter the cost and to realize it leads to everlasting life? These are a lot of questions, but I believe when you answer them, there will be freedom in your life forever. Therefore, I ask the LORD to let it rain; let it rain all YOUR promises and benefits on me. Amen.

46. Food for Thought: Thinking this morning on advancing the kingdom, it caused me to read John 15:5: "I AM the vine; you are the branches, if you remain in MEand I in you, you will bear much fruit; apart from ME you can do nothing." So then I had to ask myself what I am doing to make this happen. Fully letting all things go that does not advance HIS kingdom, the song came to me from *Frozen*, "Let it go, let it go and let JESUS grow in you, for HE is the one that can make all things possible, if we only believe!" Now, have a blessed day in the LORD, for HIS vine wants your branches to be complete.

47. Food for Thought: I'm thinking this morning on how much JESUS loves you and I, thinking how HE knew when a

sparrow fell and how much more important we are to HIM, how HE whispers in my ear and says, "I have this for you, and I will cover you today with my SPIRIT, and you will walk tall and not fall." So stand strong, for HE is there all the time, and we are made in HIS precious image. Call on the FATHER who loves us so unconditionally, and walk with a JESUS smile, for life is good. Amen.

48. Food for Thought: Have you ever noticed how a child loves to follow you around, sit on your lap, and just hang out with you, or how your dog likes to be under your feet or even sit on your lap? Well, JESUS loves us to follow HIM and to sit at HIS feet and to just hang out with HIM. JESUS is the only one who is really there all the time, day and night, 24–7; you need to be still and allow HIM to talk into your life and allow HIM to lead you. Take a deep breath, and breathe in HIS love, mercy, and grace. Amen.

49. Food for Thought: You know how we love family and friends to drop in on us, we offer them a cold drink of water or tea, and sometimes we offer them something to eat. We love the fellowship with good friends or family. When we meet new friends, we are always happy to see them or go out and eat with them for a lot of fun and good times. Well, JESUS says when we give a cold drink in HIS name or a

bite of food, we will be blessed by HIM; whatever we do to the least of them will be a blessing, and JESUS will always supply and provide what we need. Remember to smile; it's free and can change your whole outlook on life.

50. Food for Thought: Today is the day to give the LORD thanks for all HE has done for you; if you have your health, you are truly blessed. You are blessed if you have family, friends, happiness, and your needs supplied by a good job. Many are so blessed that they have all their wants also. HE is a loving FATHER like no other, but HE has a higher calling on your life, and you need to seek HIM and find out what it is. My desire is for JESUS to foster a servant's attitude in our heart, and as we call on HIM, things in our life will start to line up with HIS words for us. So start right now asking HIM to move you to a new higher level in HIM, in JESUS' name. Amen.

51. Food for Thought: If we would take the promises of GOD seriously, your life could and would be changed forever. Here is one that is great and means so much to me: "And I will bless them that bless thee, and curse Him that curseth thee: and in thee shall all the families of the earth be blessed" (Genesis 12:3; KJV). Pick up your Bible and read what the LORD has to say; HE will speak to you and

show you all HIS promises and benefits. There is a river of blessings for you when you read and then talk to JESUS. Golden nuggets wait for you, so, my precious child, talk to YOUR FATHER who loves you so very much, more than any earthly father could ever. Remember the song "Make Me a Channel of Blessings for Someone Today." Amen.

52. Food for Thought: As you pray this day, ask the LORD to give you a servant's heart, one willing to help others and to think about others more than yourself. People all over are hurting, and so many is having cancer in their families. The world needs a SAVIOR, and they need to know someone cares. Today ask GOD to bring Heaven here to earth so HIS will be done for all you lift in prayer. Remember our GOD is the Lion and the Lamb that was slain, and every knee will bow before the Lion and the Lamb. Amen.

53. Food for Thought: Have you thought about how precious the mercy and grace that GOD gives to all who are saved? Wow, I am so blessed to receive such a blessing, to know that I'm free and will live forever and be with JESUS someday soon. My heart is so full when I think about how much HE loves me and you; call on HIM today and breathe. Then be still and wait on the LORD, for HE is near and listening for your call.

54. Food for Thought: Are you tired of trying it your way and getting nowhere? Are you fully ready to turn it over to the ONE and only ONE who can make a change in your situation? All I know is that I can make a mess out of the things in life, and HE can straighten them out in a flash. All I have to do is let go and let GOD do it. I have found out just how great it is to seek the advice of the MASTER and how HE gives me wisdom, knowledge, and understanding, JESUS is a *wow* factor to me. Thank YOU, LORD. Amen.

55. Food for Thought: Have you ever thought that today is not promised to us, not even tomorrow. Well, this made me realize that when HE wakes me up, I will praise HIM; and as my day goes on, I will praise HIM; and before I go to bed at night, I will praise HIM. If your day starts out bad, just lift your voice and praise HIM; praise HIM for your family and friends, for food on your table, roof over your head, and clothes on your back. When you are in a hurry, praise HIM for all HE supplies you with and ask HIM for peace and rest; just slow down and lift your hands to praise HIM. When you change your thoughts from negative to positive, your whole body begins to feel well again. The Bible says, "In everything give thanks: for this is the will of GOD in CHRIST JESUS concerning you" (1 Thessalonians 5:18; KJV), so turn from worrying to caring for others. JESUS,

right now I give YOU praise and honor. I lift YOUR name on high, for YOU are bigger than anything here we can face. We speak what a big GOD we serve, bigger than the valleys, bigger than the sickness, bigger than any mountain, bigger than this world and everything in it! I thank YOU for covering us all the time with love, peace, and rest and holding on to us through it all. Amen.

56. Food for Thought: Have you ever heard that you will pay the price for something you have done in your life? Well, let me tell you the greatest news I know. JESUS paid the price for all of us. HE loves us that much that HE paid it in full, and we never have to pay HIM back "in whom we have redemption through HIS blood, the forgiveness of sins, according to the riches of HIS grace" (Ephesians1:7 KJV). My prayer for all is to ask JESUS into your heart today and repent of your sins and ask HIM in to stay, that is all JESUS asks of you. Who else would do this for you and me? Thank YOU, JESUS, for giving YOUR all for me. Amen.

57. Food for thought: When you read this, memorize it and watch it change your life. "Arise, shine; for thy light is come, and the glory of the LORD is risen upon thee," Isaiah 60:1 KJV. Wow these words are so powerful; think of it like this: get up and shine for the light and glory of JEHOVAH

is risen inside of you. Get up and get with it; you can do all things through HIM! So now share this good word with someone else and allow the Son shine on you forever and ever. Amen.

58. Food for Thought: As I pray and try to think about all the things that we face daily in life, I see and hear people say they are looking for hope and want to know how to stand strong in this unsettled world. I tell them they need to get in a church that still is fed by the Bible and hear what a man or woman of our living LORD has to say. Our Pastor Jay pours out His heart on what and how the HOLY SPIRIT is leading Him, and then we become partakers of this living word that waters our soul with truth. We become full as we are fed from this powerful word of GOD, so stop starving; come and eat at the MASTER's table, for it is set for you. Come and dine, and be welcomed with open arms. Amen.

59. Food for Thought: Have you ever felt like I have, and said, "One day at a time, sweet JESUS"? Well, the thing the LORD showed me was we all feel this way because we all try to plan ahead and overthink things. Sometimes we get in front of GOD instead of waiting on HIS perfect timing. So my prayer for all of us is to remember JESUS already has a plan for us, and HE has fully thought it out. Therefore,

pray and ask HIM to help you to leave it at the foot of the cross and not to pick it back up again. Ask HIM to allow you to rest in HIM and to have the faith to just believe HE has this. Amen.

60. Food for Thought: Reading the word this morning has made me realize that this world needs to know HIS promises. One of HIS great promises is found in Philippians 4:6–7 (KJV): Be careful for nothing; but in everything by prayer and supplication with thanksgiving let your request be made known unto GOD. And the peace of GOD, which passeth all understanding, shall keep your hearts and minds through CHRIST JESUS. Now do you see the big picture here and why it is important to know HIS promises, do not be anxious for nothing. HE has it covered; your part is to believe! My prayer for all who read this is to call on the name of the LORD and receive today what HE has for you. Amen.

61. Food for Thought: Have you read Ecclesiastes 3:1 (KJV): "To everything there is a season, and a time to every purpose under the heaven"; have you ever asked GOD about your season in life? This should cause you to ask GOD to show you, your purpose HE has for you. When you read all of Ecclesiastes, you will find a lot of answers to many

questions you may have had in the lesson of this thing called life. I pray you learn to love the Bible and cover yourself with HIS precious words to help build you up and fill you with all HIS benefits and promises. May HIS word become alive in you, and may you share them with others. Amen.

62. Food for Thought: There is no greater love than the love of JESUS! HIS love covers all, at all times and everywhere. HE says, "Casting all your cares on HIM, for HE careth for you" (1 Peter 5:7 KJV). So if you're trying to carry your own load, you will probably fail, for the burdens are too heavy for you alone. Turn them over to HIM, for HIS arms are open and HE will not feel the weight. HE is so ready for you today; call on HIM and trust in HIM. HE will carry you through it all. JESUS,thank YOU for loving us so and being there all the time. Amen.

About the Author

G LENDA JOHNSTON IS A wife of fifty-plus years and a mother of two sons, who are married and who have given her two beautiful daughter-in-loves, who in turn gave her three very blessed grandchildren, two precious granddaughters, one nineteen and one seventeen, and a grandson who is now twenty-three, is married, and has blessed her with a beautiful granddaughter-in-love. She also has two fur babies. Since September 2006, she has been an ordained minister but has been in the ministry for forty-plus years as a Sunday-school teacher, clerk in the church, youth leader, and young adult teacher. She had a singing ministry for thirty-five-plus years and sang with her husband and youngest son in church.

Glenda held the regional vice president position with Primerica for twenty-plus years and helped many families to become debt free and financially independent, saying "I love this company because they believed in education for the family and believed that everyone can be someone; they believed in the blue-collar worker just as much as the white collars. They believed everyone could be an owner. I have traveled all over the countryside and loved it.

Glenda says to you, "We have been very blessed through our journal of life, I have always thought, though we go through the rough waters and have gone through many, many storms in our life and sometimes my faith got so weak, but then one day it seemed as if the sun shined again, and HIS power came over me. That was when I heard the LORD say, "When you were at your weakest, I was made strong in you." See, sometimes I forgot that nothing is impossible with GOD! What a lesson I had to learn. Through this time it made me think about the word in 2 Corinthians 12:9 (NIV), "But HE said to me, 'MY grace is sufficient for you, for MY power is made perfect in weakness.' Therefore I will boast all the more gladly about my weaknesses, so that CHRIST's power may rest on me." I have seen the LORD restore us and tell us to hang on to HIM, for HE knows every detail of our lives and said, "I've been with you all the time." HE said, "I will never leave you," so we have stood on one thing.

"If it was not for the Lighthouse, where would this ship be?" So I thank GOD for the Lighthouse that has always been and will always be the light that oversees us. Who is this Lighthouse? It's JESUS! HE has seen us through it all. My heart is so full when I think of my family, church, and friends. I know in this ever-changing journey called life, I'm so thankful for HIS unchanging hand, for it never changes, what was, is, and is to come. I'm thankful for the right to do as JESUS asks me to. I'm thankful that the LORD gave me a husband who has always believed in me but more important, believed in JESUS, and was always willing to be part of these encounters in some way.

"As I put this book together, from all the notes I had made and kept through the years, my prayer is for it to spark a fire in you. May you seek JESUS and HIS love and be willing to step into the divine encounters HE may have for you. May you have a listening ear and a heart ready to receive, for we are HIS hands and feet and were made for HIM and to work until HE comes back for us. Until then, may HIS kingdom come on earth as in heaven!"

CPSIA information can be obtained
at www.ICGtesting.com
Printed in the USA
FSOW01n1426261117
41373FS

9 781545 616031